LEAVE NO BROTHER BEHIND

A Sister's War Memoir

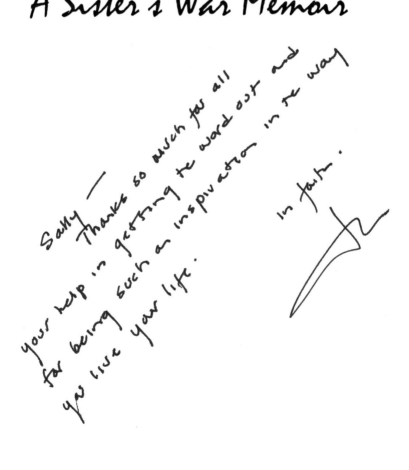

Sally —

Thanks so much for all your help in getting the word out and for being such an inspiration in the way you live your life.

In faith,

LEAVE NO BROTHER BEHIND

A Sister's War Memoir

Jan Christian

Mill City Press

MINNEAPOLIS

Mill City Press, Inc.

212 3rd Avenue North, Suite 290

Minneapolis, MN 55401

612.455.2294

www.millcitypublishing.com

Cover photo of Bobby and Jan Christian by Maxine Christian.

Excerpts from *The Vietnam Experience: A War Remembered.* New York, Time Life, 1986, used courtesy of The Boston Publishing Co.; "The Boy Was Young" by Rudolph W. Nemser used courtesy of his estate.

ISBN - 978-1-936400-49-2

ISBN - 1-936400-49-9

LCCN - 2010935696

Cover Design by Alan Pranke

Typeset by James Arneson

Printed in the United States of America

Dedication

For 2nd Lt. Robert M. Christian, Jr. (Bobby)
and his Marine Brothers of Kilo Company,
Third Battalion, First Marines (K/3/1)

How could it be otherwise?

Somewhere underneath all the politics, the ambition, the harsh talk, the power, the violence, the will to destroy and waste and maim and burn, was this tenderness. Tenderness born into madness, preservable only by suffering, and finally not preservable at all. What can love do? Love waits, if it must, maybe forever.

Wendell Berry, *Jayber Crow*

PART I
Separation

Chapter 1

Down, down, down into the darkness of the grave
Gently they go, the beautiful, the tender, the kind;
Quietly they go, the intelligent, the witty, the brave.
I know. But I do not approve. And I am not
resigned.

Edna St. Vincent Millay

May 15, 2008. My brother's sixty-third birthday. I propose a toast. "For Bobby, the best older brother anyone ever had. His life shaped my life in ways both subtle and profound, and his death is changing my life still. And to his Marine brothers, those of you gathered here and those far away. You have taught me about faithfulness and what it really means to leave no brother behind."

It was my mother who answered the door around dusk on an April evening in 1969. She took one look at the two men there and said, "It's Bobby."

There are times when the body understands immediately what the mind takes months to grasp. The body knows the earth has shifted, but the mind seeks the still horizon. My father, hearing her from a nearby room, thought what he wanted to think, what he had to think: *Bobby is back. He's come home.*

Four months earlier, I drove my dad and brother in our family car, a '65 white Barracuda with red interior, from our home in Boulder City, Nevada to the Las Vegas airport. I was a month short of having my license. Maybe Dad didn't trust himself behind the wheel. My mother stayed home; she couldn't be part of it.

I pulled up to the curb and got to the back of the car as my brother, stiff in his Marine uniform, lifted his bag out. I must have hugged him. Dad stuck out his hand and said, "Don't be a hero." Back in the car, looking straight ahead, he said, "We have the happiest day of our life to look forward to—the day he comes home." I turned the key.

The Marines had delivered the news and gone by the time I got home. Our house was on a hill, and Dad was waiting for me in the darkness at the bottom of the driveway. When I was three, he had waited in a different driveway with that same look. Then, my sister, Florence, had polio.

Before I could get to his arms, he spoke two words. "Bobby's dead."

Bobby. The one who hung the moon. The center. Gone.

"I know," I said and ran into the darkness.

The day he comes home. As we waited for the telegram and the details it would provide, I thought of a joke Bobby often told. The recipient of a telegram gushes, "Oh, I have always wanted a singing telegram." The guy delivering the telegram is stricken. "Ma'am, this is not a singing telegram." She insists. Reluctantly, he sings it. "Your sister, Rose, is dead."

My mother, our minister Rev. Holliday, and I were out front when the first telegram arrived. We huddled together reading it. My eyes rushed over the misspellings and the incomplete sentences.

"What is this?" Mom tapped a word on the telegram with her finger. "What is this word?"

I went back to see. The word was misspelled. Without considering the impact, I said, "'Unviewable.' The word is supposed to be 'unviewable.'"

She began to fold upon herself, and our minister, who was not much bigger than Mom was, reached out to steady her. I turned and walked away.

4

While we waited, I ate. I sat at the kitchen table welcoming the food that temporarily filled me. There were others around the table. My friend Carolyn Wagner came that first night to drive me around town until the tears were depleted. Stewart Bell, my brother's best friend since elementary school, was there. As we played cards, Stewart and his brother John told a story about an ugly dog they saw on their way to the house. They speculated about the possibility that digs or pogs exist since this thing looked like a cross between a pig and a dog.

Though it felt strange, laughter was the perfect tribute to my brother, and the kitchen was just the place for it. It was there, years earlier, I succeeded in making Bobby, who was eight years older, pass milk through his nose. Life didn't get better than that.

My cousin Lucile, who was slightly older than my mother, heard the laughter and came to tell us that playing cards and laughing was inappropriate "at a time like this." I was already learning about the different ways people grieve. Some grow silent as socks; some can't stop talking. Some get busy, looking for salvation in the details; some are impatient with all things trivial. Lucile and a few others had fixed ideas about the right way and the wrong way to grieve. To hell with their rules and with them. I didn't have to convince anyone of my love for my brother or of my grief over his death. Some folks just get angry.

When musician Boz Scaggs lost his son, he said that it was as if his world exploded and he didn't recognize the pieces. Different pieces kept floating to earth that week, and I had no idea where to put them or how they fit together or what picture, if any, they might create.

My sister, Florence, flew down from Palo Alto, where she and her family were spending the year while her husband finished a Ph.D. at Stanford. She brought a poem that Bobby wrote and she had received after he died but in the hours before we heard. *My brother wrote poetry?* It was not something he would have sent to our parents.

5

Ambush

The orange sun slips to its grave.
Four young men prepare to fight,
The jungle smothered in darkness,
Invisible forms slip through the night.

Beside the trail they halt, silent . . . alert.
Minutes into hours, wet, cold to the bone.
Waiting . . .waiting . . .waiting . . .wait!
A sound, barely audible. A turned stone?

Ready! Fire!
Muzzles crash, red, orange, white.
Blinding flashes in the dark, then silence. . . .
Victory! All nine lie still in our sight.

The sun breaks clear
Burning away the mist,
The ambush returns
at funeral pace.
Three men carry a lifeless form.
This is victory? Victory?! In what race?

In March, Bobby wrote that he was taking a job in the rear and that mom could stop worrying. If he felt this way about what he was doing, why did he go back into the bush?

There were more revelations. According to my sister, Bobby had called dad from Quantico, Virginia and told him that the whole thing was crazy and he wanted out and was even willing to go to Canada. My dad called a cousin's husband, an Army colonel, and said, "Go talk some sense into that boy." He wasn't supposed to be a hero, but deserter wasn't an option, either.

Bobby had also written from Quantico that he had a good chance of going to language school in Monterey, California. This was great news, but he never mentioned it again. That week we learned that he gave his spot to a friend. This same friend, when hearing of Bobby's death, promised us that, if he ever had a son, he would name him after my brother.

Bobby had $10,000 in life insurance and a policy that would pay off the loan on his new silver Datsun 2000 convertible sports car. He had left the car in my care, saying, "I have more faith that I will come home in one piece than that this car will be in one piece when I get back." The car was at least viewable at the end of the year. My parents decided I could keep the car. My sister would be given something else, and they would have the money, but then word came that I was the sole beneficiary of the insurance money. He was still looking out for me.

Bobby came home.

My mother, sister, and I went to the mortuary; Dad couldn't be part of it. My cousin Bonnie Belle, the wife of that Army colonel, told me that if my parents really wanted to see my brother's body, they could insist. I didn't even consider telling them.

So, without her son's body, my mother patted the grey metal casket and spoke snatches of sentences as if comforting a fitful baby. My sister's hand moved up and down her back. Some poor kid in uniform stood guard. Talk about hazardous duty. Probably nothing in boot camp or beyond prepared him for my mother's grief. Suddenly, she turned and looked at him, as if for the first time. A young man in uniform. Her hands slowly reached out to touch him. He stood ramrod straight, eyes straight ahead, like the guards I had seen at the Tomb of the Unknown Soldier. I walked away as she found her baby.

It was my first funeral. I stuffed my body, now ten pounds heavier than before my brother's death, into a white dress with embroidered flowers. A Marine honor guard flanked the church entrance so I held back. The Marine Corps represented what took my brother away, piece by piece, leaving something unfit for human viewing. After boot camp, something in my brother was hidden.

He came home twenty pounds heavier and more self-contained. He still called me by my nickname, Tico. We still shared an easy physicality. When I leaned against him, he still draped an arm around my shoulder, but something had changed. The Marines dispersed, and we entered. Stewart kept his sunglasses on, but I didn't need sunglasses because I wasn't going to cry.

At the cemetery, I focused on how to keep from going crazy when they lowered the casket into the ground. In spite of my discomfort with public displays of grief, I imagined following him into the hole. Barely aware of words being spoken, I focused on the flag-draped casket and the hole. The casket. The hole. I was only a few feet away and would have a straight shot.

The flag was removed and folded precisely. No loose ends there. A Marine took the flag in both of his white-gloved hands, walked to where my mother sat, bent slightly, and offered it to her. She placed it in her lap and rested both hands on it as if to keep it from floating away.

Then the service was over without the casket being lowered, but the question remained: How was I going to keep from going crazy? And, given the circumstances, what exactly was crazy? Does normal exist in the midst of insanity?

It was a Saturday afternoon, a lovely spring day. People followed us up the hill to our house which looked out on the desert and to Lake Mead, where we spent so much time as a family.

As I passed by my father, he turned to a friend and said, "*She's* the one who would have made a good Marine."

I kept walking. What the hell did that mean? That I was tough? Yes, that was true and they hadn't seen anything yet. Did it mean my brother, who was good at everything, was not good at being a Marine? Was he not a good Marine because he got shot in the head? Was he not a good Marine because he was so gentle and loving and kind? Was he not a good Marine because he realized that he was killing for something that didn't make any sense? Why the hell would anyone want a child to be a Marine, good or otherwise? How can you send someone—no, not just *someone*, your *son*—to war and tell them to not be a hero but expect them to be a good Marine?

Weeks later, my dad and I were on that same stretch of road between Las Vegas and Boulder City. At Railroad Pass, where small desolate hills spread out from the highway, I surprised myself by speaking the words I was thinking.

"It's a good thing I'm not a boy because I wouldn't have gone," I said.

"If I had a hundred sons," he said, "they would all go."

My dad had two heart attacks before my birth and always carried nitroglycerine. Once he took my brother deer hunting and my brother got lost. Although he was only about twelve, he propped himself up against a tree all night long, afraid that if he lay down to sleep, my father would come across him, think he had been shot, and have a heart attack.

One evening after my brother's death, my dad was missing. We spread out to look for him, worried that his heart had stopped. I found him lying in the front yard, whimpering. My father was almost 6'3" and over two hundred pounds, so I held onto both of his hands and coaxed him up, leaning back with all my weight. He lumbered up and lurched a bit when I let go of his hands, so I wrapped my arm around his right arm and led him to his bed. He just kept repeating, "They've killed my boy. They've killed my boy."

How many of those one hundred sons did he think he could bury before his heart gave out?

Chapter 2

If God's on our side
He'll stop the next war.

Bob Dylan

When I was four, I stood in the surf holding my father's hand as the sand disappeared beneath my feet with each wave. Suddenly, I was down. I came up sputtering, and the pound of sand and small sea creatures in the crotch of my bathing suit did nothing to improve my mood. I cast an angry eye on my dad and demanded to know why he let me down.

"Tico, I was knocked down, too," he answered.

I never considered the possibility that there were things that could knock my father down.

We were all down with no idea how to get ourselves back up, let alone how to reach a hand out to one another. In the week after my brother's death, our large house was filled with relatives. I awoke in the middle of the night, walked into the living room and found my father sitting on the couch.

"It's going to be hard when they are all gone," he said.

Now they were gone, and presumably life was supposed to go on and in much the same way that it had always gone on. Carolyn's family always had a jigsaw puzzle on a card table and even though I knew how they were supposed to look when they were finished, I was hopeless at identifying the right piece for the right spot. My life was now a jigsaw puzzle with no picture on the box.

My still immortal peers had other things on their minds and were largely unprepared to deal with a friend on a death trip. It's unclear how I might have responded to an adult who was equipped to deal with a grieving teen or even a grieving adult, but I didn't get much chance to find out.

Bobby had graduated at the top of his high school class. Mrs. Mitchell, who was to become my senior English teacher, came to our house when Bobby died and wisely shared tears with us instead of platitudes or her own strong religious beliefs. But there were some who were like the visitors who come to your hospital bed to tell you about their own botched surgery or to claim their illness was the worst the doctors had ever seen. One woman told my mother, "They say it gets better and that time heals all wounds, but that isn't true. It never gets better." My mother never forgot that line.

One after another, adults embraced me and said, "You have to be strong for your parents." They didn't say who was going to be strong for me, and, for all I knew, they were telling my parents they had to be strong for me. No one wanted us to be real.

Another response was, "Oh, was he your *only* brother?" I was always tempted to answer, "No, I have a few more at home just like him." When I said that he was, they answered, "Oh that *is* sad."

"Now he will be forever young," was another classic. Gee, with an option like death, why was anyone looking for a Fountain of Youth?

And then there was the standard: "It was God's will."

The Grace Community Church in Boulder City was a central part of my childhood. My best friend Susan, the minister's daughter, moved to town just before I did, and we gravitated to one another as new kids often do. One day after school, she took me to see the church. I had never been in such a place when it was empty. We toured the labyrinth of buildings and rooms and then entered the main sanctuary from the back. I was delighted by the baptismal pool, hidden under the floor, unused by this congregation. From the pulpit, I looked out over the darkened rows of pews illuminated only by the late afternoon light filtering through the stained glass windows.

The children worshipped in a separate little chapel before going to class. My mother often sang what I later knew to be Negro spirituals, and here my knowledge and love of hymns expanded. Over the years, I had both my brother and my sister as Sunday school teachers and I taught a class while still a teenager. Bobby taught my high school class when he was in college even though he was working full time and had petitioned to take twenty-one credits.

For years I volunteered in the infant/toddler room during the second service, protecting the babies from the large, simple-minded woman in spike heels who was paid to be there. After she told me that she had accidentally stepped on a kitten and killed it, I became particularly vigilant when children crawled near her rocking chair.

Prior to confirmation, a dozen of us gathered before school for donuts and hot chocolate and discussions with the minister. Mostly I remember Tex trying to set a donut-eating record, which didn't seem to impress the minister as much as it did the rest of us. For our last class, the minister invited us to paint a picture of God. Only years later did I realize what a radical act that was in a world where people kill and die defending their images of God or their opposition to images of their God.

As we painted, he told us the story of a teacher who asks a little boy what he is painting. "I am painting a picture of God," he responds. The teacher laughs. "No one knows what God looks like," she says. "Well," the little boy answers, "they will as soon as I'm done." I intended for my picture to be all dark with a ray of light shining through, but it ended up being mostly sunshine.

And now I was supposed to believe that my brother's death was God's plan. Rather than comfort me, the idea scared and alienated me. How exactly did these people come to know about God's plan? Could it be that we were actually thwarting God's plan by killing one another? Is whatever stupid thing we do to ourselves or others part of God's plan? If so, whatever happened to free will? If we really are not free to choose good or evil, how can we be judged by God based on our actions? On the other hand, if God really sent his own son to die, why not my brother? If God is all powerful and all knowing and can intervene in daily affairs, it follows that either God willed my brother to die or, at least, didn't will him to live. Why would I worship a God like that?

The other standard response was, "He died for his country, and his death was not in vain." Perhaps my brother's willingness to answer his country's call was honorable, but what about the call itself?

I was predisposed to question decisions of our government since two of my three former foster sisters were victimized first by their families and then by the system that was supposed to protect them. Annie came to live with us when we were both four.[1] She came only with the clothes she wore—baggy brown corduroy pants and a ratty red sweater—and she whimpered as she was led to where Mom and I sat on folding chairs. She and I were day and night. She was tiny for her age and had long, stringy brown hair pulled back in a ponytail and cut in a weird way over her ears, and I was tall and almost white-haired, with a page-boy haircut.

Annie showed all the classic signs of neglect, although I didn't understand that then. Ants trailed to her bottom drawer seeking the left-over cinnamon toast she hoarded. When not watched, she ate to the point of vomiting, which we found out the hard way on the way home from a church potluck. Mom got her out of the car just in time, but she threw up all over her sneakers.

The next-to-youngest of nine or so kids, she knew how to fight and was dangerous when cornered. One Sunday morning,

---

1   The names of my foster sisters have been changed.

we got into a fight and, in just seconds, we were on the ground, her feet pushing on my shoulders and her hands pulling fistfuls of my hair. Dad saved my life, or at least what remained of my hair, by saying, "I am ashamed of the two of you for fighting. And on a Sunday morning!" I preferred dishonor over death (or even hair loss).

She told about being left alone with the baby and not being tall enough to reach the light switch when it grew dark. She picked places in our house where she could hide if "they" came to get her. One day, we came home from kindergarten to find Mom in our room ironing Annie's dresses. Without looking up, she said, in a falsely chipper way, "Annie is going home the day after tomorrow!"

The three of us went to an abandoned gas station in North Las Vegas for the hand-off. Annie's mother, whom she had said was beautiful, was a dead-ringer for the Wicked Witch of the West. Annie stood between Mom and me and I held her hand and tried, unsuccessfully, not to cry. Her mother tentatively approached her and told her that she had a new baby doll waiting for her at home. Annie's hand slipped out of mine. The baby doll was the latest addition to the family. Annie had two babies to care for. At least now she could reach the light switch.

My second foster sister, Roberta, arrived with boxes of personal items and loads of emotional baggage. She had flunked kindergarten, which I didn't know was possible. She told us to call her John, and she wore flannel shirts and long pants even when it was over a hundred degrees. Mom convinced our principal, Mr. Mitchell, to allow her to go into first grade. I was years older and so we played school when she got home.

The welfare department leaked her location, and the mother's boyfriend showed up at the school, looking for her. Because her safety was compromised, child welfare removed her just before Christmas. On January seventeenth, my birthday, they called and asked if we would take her back. I stood by the window waiting, but she never came. The people in charge of protecting her had changed their minds.

So I knew my government was not infallible, but there was nothing I wanted more than to find justification for my brother's death. As I read about the history of Vietnam and our involvement, my disappointment grew. There were people who thought we belonged in Vietnam but thought we were making strategic mistakes. We weren't fighting it aggressively enough or giving our military leaders the latitude they needed. Given the level of destruction, I wasn't sure what that latitude would look like. Others thought we didn't belong there in the first place and that China, Japan, and France hadn't belonged there either, and that if we had two brain cells to rub together, we might have learned something about their failures in Vietnam and stayed the hell out. Some thought we were backing the wrong side. Some thought we were the wrong side. A few others, like the Buddhist monks, took a radical approach against war itself. These people really scared other people because they didn't seem to be on anyone's side.

My teachers chose me to go to Girls State that summer of 1969. Bobby had gone to Boys State seven years earlier, and I was pleased to follow in his footsteps. Later that summer, I was one of two girls sent from Nevada to Girls Nation in Washington, D.C. During the visit to the United States Marine Corps War Memorial, better known as the Iwo Jima Memorial, I came undone. I sat alone on the bus crying while others walked through the cemetery with its thousands of white headstones in neat rows. A black girl, maybe the only one there, returned to the bus and sat next to me.

"That woman was telling us how beautiful this is," she said. "Thousands of men dead from war. That's beautiful? I don't think so."

I didn't think so either.

Girls State and Girls Nation were programs of the American Legion Auxiliary aimed at promoting a love of God and country. For the first time, I questioned that alliance and my allegiance. I knew there were religious people who didn't think God supported war, but I began to notice that religion and flag-waving nationalism seemed to go hand-in-hand for most people. The children's chapel at our church had a Christian flag in one corner and an American flag in the other, and we said a pledge to both.

It was just assumed that God was on our side, and any questioning of this made people angry. This part I didn't get. My mom sometimes said to me, "I love you, but I hate your low down ways." I understood this, both the logic and the part about my low down ways, so it made sense to me that I could love my country and my church and still hate their low down ways, but many others, my dad included, didn't share my logic. That fall, as a senior, I got my only unexcused absence for participating in the War Moratorium rally at the University of Nevada at Las Vegas. When Dad heard about it, he said, "If I ever find out that you have marched behind a Viet Cong flag, I will either kill you or myself." Although I had no intention of doing such a thing, instead of reassuring him, I responded, "I hope it is yourself."

I visited the cemetery on a national holiday. Some organization was putting little American flags and tacky Styrofoam crosses on each veteran's grave as if there was no disconnect between what the two required or sanctioned. When I removed them, someone had the bad sense to confront me. I had the bad sense to confront them. And so it went.

Dad once told someone that he put his faith in "God, country, and family." And to my surprise, he added, with emphasis, "*in that order.*" My mother remained silent about God and country. One afternoon I came home and found her sobbing on her bed. As I tried to comfort her, she said. "If it wasn't for your father needing me, I would kill myself."

Chapter 3

The Boy Was Young

The boy was young (your son, my son).
He held life,
gentle and fragile as a wren's spotted egg,
in play-black-lined hands.

He brought it to me.
His eyebrows asked: What?
How should this find,
this all-that-he-had,
glistening in its bed of dark sweat
be used?
What does it mean
to hold your life with your fingers?

How should I tell him how to live?
How do you tell someone you love
humanity is frail
(as he is frail, as you are frail)
and mistakes will be made
and life is fitting parts that don't belong?

Rudolph W. Nemser

Since Bobby left his car in my care, I argued with my parents that the car, now paid for, should belong to me. They sold it to me for $2,500, leaving me with a convertible sports car and $7,500. Years before, Bobby had told me he would pay my college expenses, but instead he bought me my independence, and my parents, in their grief, handed over what he couldn't buy.

Within months, we sold our house with five-and-a-half bathrooms and bought a double-wide trailer in a mobile home park where we had lived for a while when we first moved to Nevada. Mom had to get out of the house and even out of town. My father took an early medical retirement at age sixty-three. This wasn't difficult because he had two heart attacks and tuberculosis in both lungs before I was born. A few years before, he had a stroke from which he recovered. They left just before Thanksgiving of my senior year in high school and didn't return until early January. They were gone again on the anniversary of Bobby's death.

Looking back now, as a parent, it seems an act of extreme neglect or foolishness, but it felt like liberation then. My own sadness was heavy enough without carrying theirs. To grieve with others can divide our grief or multiply it. Mine felt multiplied in the presence of my parents and divided in the presence of my sister, who shared my questions and whose mental health I didn't rely on.

Christmas was a major holiday in our family, and I worked hard that year to get in the spirit. My friends Wayne, Denise, and Carolyn borrowed Denise's mom's station wagon, which had a luggage rack on top, and we all went shopping for a Christmas tree for me. Wayne asked the guy to tie the tree upright on top of the car. The poor guy was struggling with a response when he heard our laughter from the next row. On our way home, the tree actually stood upright—just before it flew off in the middle of Charleston Boulevard. We decorated the top with a hand flipping a peace sign that Wayne crafted out of florescent orange poster board, and we spray painted peace signs in the front windows with canned snow.

In November of 1968, Bobby had written, "I have some good news and some bad news. I will be seeing Bob Hope for Christmas." This was the time of year he should have been coming home. It wasn't the first time that I had fantasized that he hadn't really been killed, but this fantasy grew as the holidays grew closer. We hadn't seen the body. Maybe he deserted and someone else's body was put in his place. There were places where deserters hung out in Vietnam. Maybe he walked out of Vietnam. What would he look like all scruffy and overgrown? What if I came face to face with him and didn't even recognize him? I considered the possibility that he might see me and not acknowledge me. I wondered what he would think if he showed up at our house and we were all gone, as if he could have walked out of Vietnam but might not have been able to find us across town. I walked the old neighborhood, half expecting to see him. Of course it didn't make sense; grief is not bound by logic.

Most people didn't want to talk about death and grief. Some were "too sensitive." They claimed this as if it was a good thing, even though it seemed to mean they were sensitive only to their own feelings. Some saw it as their job to help us get over our grief as if it were simply a hurdle on the track of life. They avoided anything that might remind us, as if we might otherwise be able to forget. Although people tried to shield us from reminders, images of war and the ravages of war were everywhere. These reminders didn't deepen my grief; they forced others to share it, and that seemed only fair.

Although the clichés designed to comfort or appease just irritated me, it was words that saved me. Through reading, I came to know that my experience of suffering was not only personal, but universal.

In sixth grade, I had faced junior high with trepidation (and not just because of having to shower with all the other girls). "How can I be prepared for it?" I asked my brother.

"Read," he answered.

"Read what?"

"Read everything and anything," he said.

"I already do that."

"Then you will be fine."

My light blue library card with the metal strip was well worn. Although this was my first significant personal experience with death, I had read, maybe to an unnatural extent, about death:

books by black authors filled with unfair and violent deaths and everything written about the Kennedy assassination and its aftermath. It was another Bobby who helped save me. Bobby Kennedy had also struggled with grief over the death of an older brother and been changed in the struggle. Jacqueline Kennedy suggested he read the Greek tragedies. He came to favor a piece by Aeschylus which became his epitaph:

> He who learns must suffer
> And even in our sleep pain that cannot forget
> Falls drop by drop upon the heart,
> And in our own despair, against our will,
> Comes wisdom to us by the awful grace of God.[1]

Like Bobby Kennedy, I read the Greek tragedies and Tennyson, who wrote about unexpected tears that rise "from the depth of some divine despair" and promised that it was "not too late to seek a newer world." I, too, read "Letters to a German Friend," in which Albert Camus took his friend to task for not questioning Germany's role in World War II. He wrote, "I should like to be able to love my country and still love justice. I don't want any greatness for it, particularly a greatness born of blood and falsehood. I want to keep it alive by keeping justice alive." Camus got the same response I got: You don't really love your country.

I also read *Death Be Not Proud*, *A Separate Peace*, *All Quiet on the Western Front* and *Johnny Got His Gun*. The ending of *The Catcher in the Rye* caught me by surprise because Holden seemed so like me. Was I losing it too?

Just weeks after my brother's death, my English teacher, Mr. Wyndham, stood by my desk and read Alan Seeger's poetry from World War I.

---

1   Kennedy's variation of a passage in Aeschylus's *Agamemnon*.

I have a rendezvous with Death
At some disputed barricade,
When Spring comes back with rustling shade
And apple-blossoms fill the air—
I have a rendezvous with Death
When Spring brings back blue days and fair.[2]

My brother had not only written a poem before his death, he had been reading poetry by Rod McKuen, who wrote of war and giving the other side a chance and the unshakable sadness that clings to those who have killed. I wondered what my brother would have been like had he survived the war. One of his classmates, Roy Legler, who also went to Boys State and attended our church, went to Vietnam. Not long after returning, he left a note for the Police Chief, who lived next door, took his car out into the desert, and attached a vacuum cleaner hose to the exhaust pipe.

Some of the words that saved me were set to music. Bobby's favorite memories from boot camp included a guy who did a great James Brown impersonation and a day when they cranked up the Beatles during kitchen duty and everyone mopped and swept to "You say you want a revolution."[3] His Christmas gifts to me were often records. From Vietnam, he wrote a family friend that he had a collection of four hundred albums and six hundred singles. I don't know where all of them went after his death, but the few that made it into my hands were like gifts chosen by him for me. I had heard Simon and Garfunkel, but I had not held *The Sounds of Silence* in my hands. I listened to the words and felt known. They sang of feeling like an island, of darkness as a friend and of pretending that hopes can be rebuilt.

Here were people who had known anger at injustice and had suffered. My anger and suffering were not greater than theirs. I

---

2   Alan Seeger, *Poems.* 1917.
3   John Lennon, "Revolution." *The Beatles*, Apple Records, 1968.

didn't have the words, but they did. They showed me that there is life after death. It wasn't the life after death that my childhood religion promised, but the here and now kind of life. It was not life as it was before, but it was life. And it, too, could be beautiful.

Our grieving as a family was mostly solitary and took us down different paths. As a younger sibling, I avoided the guilt that plagues parents and often older siblings regardless of the circumstances and, even then, I knew this was a gift. We faced the days in different ways, but we each awoke, dressed, and put one foot in front of the other. The times we judged one another harshly were few and far between. We each would speak differently about faith and the meaning of my brother's death, but whatever our differences, we were each keeping faith with life in the midst of death. And even when our differences were raw, we learned to say "I love you" to one another. Over time, we learned not to let arguments linger too long, knowing now that any goodbye could be the last.

Grief is not linear; it doesn't follow a straight line. The path is filled with unexpected twists and turns, an anticipated shortcut ends up being a dead end. The path seems to clear, only to turn rugged. But after two years, my grief was no longer "it." My brother's death went from being some horrific thing out there to such a part of my being that I could not separate myself from it or imagine who I would be had he lived. Sadness would come, of course, but the exhausting work of grief was over.

I took one of Bobby's wool pullover sweaters when he died. It had horizontal stripes of various shades of brown. One night, some friends pushed me in a pool while I was wearing it and as it dried it got smaller and smaller. I felt guilty and sad and was reluctant to part with it even though it no longer fit. Eventually I let it go, knowing that I would always remember how it felt to wear it. My grief was like that sweater.

But grief and guilt still moved through others in ways unknown to me.

Chapter 4

Going home must be like going to render an account.

Joseph Conrad

I moved to Arizona in 1973, and my parents soon followed. My sister had moved to nearby Las Vegas, and then on to Pittsburgh.

Watergate shook Dad's faith in his country and visibly aged him. His government lied to him. Nixon had not only lied, but allowed his daughter to defend him, knowing his own guilt. My father saw Nixon's betrayal of his child as worse than his betrayal of his country. Perhaps "God, Country, and Family" wasn't really in that order. Richard Nixon resigned in disgrace in August, 1974, and in September, President Gerald Ford pardoned him, saying, "I do believe, with all my heart and mind and spirit, that I, not as President but as a humble servant of God, will receive justice without mercy if I fail to show mercy." He told us that "Richard Nixon and his loved ones have suffered enough and will continue to suffer, no matter what I do, no matter what we, as a great and good nation, can do together to make his goal of peace come true."

Dad went out in front of his little house in Leisure World in Mesa, Arizona, and hung the American flag upside down, a traditional signal of distress. When President Ford offered a conditional opportunity for pardon to draft evaders and deserters, Dad had no comment.

Dad died of cancer in 1978 and we took his ashes to Boulder City to bury them next to Bobby.

Although Rev. Holliday was no longer the minister at Grace Community Church, he officiated at my dad's small grave-side service. I held it together until I saw Susan and her mother, Jean, coming towards us. Jean was a favorite of my dad's. They once went fishing together, and it was hard to know if he got a bigger kick out of her or the idea of taking the minister's wife out. Rev. Holliday had read from Ecclesiastes: "There is a time for every purpose under heaven. A time for peace, a time for war." I still didn't understand how there could be a time for war.

Guy and Jean Holliday had buried a grandchild by then. Susan, Jean, and I walked together through the cemetery, remembering people along the way. As we stood over her grandson's grave, Jean said that it doesn't make any sense to give in to grief. There is nothing to be gained by it.

Two years later, in 1980, I returned to Boulder City for my ten-year high school reunion, a reunion that set a pattern for subsequent reunions. The first night we gathered at a classmate's house, and the next day we decorated a float for the Fourth of July parade and then had a banquet dinner. On the Fourth, we rode on the float and later gathered at the park for the festivities.

I saw Susan Holliday that first night of the reunion. She told me that, after my brother's death, her father had experienced a crisis of faith. Perhaps the easy certainty I had observed in people was more bluster than fact. I wished I had known then because some doubt shared along the way would have reassured me; it was the easy certainty of people that left me feeling alienated and adrift.

Ten years passed between reunions. Even if I had used those years to contemplate what new revelations might await, I would never have guessed. On that first night of my twentieth reunion, in 1990, I stood in Mike Shipp's kitchen drinking a beer.

"Have you ever seen the *Time Life* series on Vietnam?" he asked.

"I've heard of it," I said, "but haven't seen the books."

"I think there might be an article about your brother's death in one of them. I loaned it to Paul, but he could go get it if you want to see it."

Thirty minutes later, Paul and Mike walked me into a spare bedroom, exchanged glances, handed me *The Vietnam Experience: A War Remembered*[1] opened to the right page, and hurried out. The first paragraph ended, "Well, this was no firefight we were in on April 11, 1969. It was a total, all-out battle and it haunted me for years and years."

According to one Stephen W. Gregory, the day before the firefight, they were digging up enemy graves and so they didn't have a chance to get set up and prepare for the night. They were hit all night long and took multiple casualties. Gregory figured that the next morning they would send an entire platoon out, but the order came to send one squad, and so he took the order to my brother, who was the 2nd Platoon commander.

Bobby picked Alpha squad, led by Gregory's best friend, Johnnie Lee (J. L.) Anderson. Gregory was the platoon radioman and insisted that he wanted to carry the radio for the squad because J. L.'s radioman had not been in-country long. Gregory said that when Bobby disagreed, "I just looked at him and said, 'Fuck you. I'm going with Alpha.'"

When you're a boot officer who's only been in country four days and you look at this nineteen-year-old kid who looks like he's been through about thirty wars, with that stare that says he's been there for a while, it's very difficult to say no. Because he's liable to just shoot you where you stand! So anyway, I disobeyed his orders and went ahead and carried the radio for Alpha Squad. I knew we were going to get hit.

1   Clark Dougan, David Fulghum, and Dennis Kennedy. *The Vietnam Experience: A War Remembered*. New York, Time Life, 1986, 176–181.

I had read enough Vietnam memoirs and novels to know about the pervasive mistrust of 2nd Lieutenants, who were often rotated to the rear by the time they were no longer considered green, but Bobby had been in Vietnam since just before Christmas of 1968. For one of the few times in my life, I felt a desire to defend the brother who always defended me.

A disjointed account followed. The squad was soon in a "semi-circle ambush." J. L. was hit immediately and "probably took two or three rounds in the stomach, because he was pulling at himself and rolling and yelling 'Corpsman! Corpsman! Corpsman!'"

Gregory's radio was hit so he couldn't transmit, but he was in touch with Lt. Hobbs, the company commander, by clicking his headset to answer yes or no to questions. Three other guys were badly wounded and "one guy's arm was nearly gone." Gregory kept trying to get to J. L., but then a Chicom[2] landed near J. L. "In his pain and anguish he rolled so much that he rolled right over onto the Chicom, and that just blew him the hell away."

Even though the entire squad had gone out, Gregory wrote, "I was in there for another three and a half hours, just by myself. I went to every last one of the others and patched up those that I could patch up. I used every grenade that anybody was carrying." Suddenly, my brother reappeared in the narrative:

> Then Lt. Christian decided he was going to make a run in there to help us out. So he came in and got down on my left side on one knee, John Wayne-style, to throw a grenade. Luckily he threw the grenade first as he got shot right between the eyes. It was the fastest death I'd ever seen during the entire time I was in Vietnam. His eyes just closed and he flopped over and he was dead. Then minutes later the 3rd Platoon's lieutenant, Lieutenant Peterson, did the same thing on the right side of me and got shot through the face.

---

2   Chinese Communist grenade.

Somehow, another platoon leader had appeared. Although wounded, Gregory "went back into the ambush to retrieve the dead and wounded," getting help from others only after "the third or fourth guy." He continued:

> The worst thing in the world was picking up J. L. with nothing left of him from his chin to his crotch but a small portion of intestines hanging out, the rest of him just totally blown away. His eyes were wide open. He died a very, very horrific death. You could see it in his eyes, he died in pure pain.

Gregory wished that he had "died a normal death, like Lieutenant Christian—one round through the head."

Although wounded, he and two guys then "went bunker to bunker with hand grenades." He "pulled wounded gooks out of the bunkers and shot them in the head" and then called in Phantom jets and two tanks. For this, he claimed to have been awarded the Bronze Star.

Three weeks after Gregory got home, he punched out a guy who called him a "baby killer" and was sentenced in civilian court to eighteen months in a maximum-security prison and then was given "an undesirable discharge." The ambush continued to haunt him, and he had more run-ins with the law.

In 1977, he walked into a bank in Silver Spring, Maryland, and took hostages. His insanity defense didn't work, and he received a sixteen-year sentence. He was eventually granted a new trial and pled guilty to reduced charges. "The VA was there to say that they had screwed up on my case and that I should have received treatment all the way back in 1970 when I first went to them. Two doctors testified on my behalf," he wrote. He was given probation.

He got into another fight with someone who disrespected him, and in the car chase with police, a girl was killed. He was sent to prison where he got active in veteran's issues and helped vets in prison get help for damage related to Agent Orange and Post-Traumatic Stress Disorder (PTSD). He was one of the first

veterans to be awarded compensation for PTSD and to success-
fully use it as a defense in a criminal case. At the end of the article,
there was a picture of Gregory with his wife, taken in 1985.

By then I had worked for fifteen years in and around Arizona's
social service and justice systems, and I recognized this guy and
others like him who always cast themselves as victims or heroes, or
both, in their own stories. He clearly had serious problems when
he went to Vietnam, and the experiences of war, including watching his best friend die a horrendous death that day, did nothing to
improve his mental health. I was sorry for him, but sorrier that my
brother died next to him.

A surreal quality hung over the rest of the reunion. Images,
which rested just under the surface during the day, appeared as
soon as I closed my eyes to sleep. I had pictured the bullet hitting
Bobby on the right side of his head and was strangely troubled by
Gregory's report that the bullet hit him between the eyes.

Later I showed the article to my husband, Michael Roach,
who enlisted in the Marines at age seventeen and did two tours in
Vietnam. I also sent it to my sister who, in return, sent me some
memories from that time and a copy of an article she published
not long after our brother's death. In it she quoted Lt. H. Larry
Klein who knew Bobby at Quantico:

> There is no patriotism in this war. All we're doing is trying to
> protect each other and stay alive. Men like Lieutenant Bob come
> along once in a million years. We both knew that our survival
> depended upon two things: the ability of our men and politics.
> Bob made his men the best. He did his part. We all are. We are
> waiting for that other half...All we can do, as the Marines say, is
> remember and continue to march. I am proud to say that once in
> my lifetime, I had a brother.

I never told my mother about the article and, even if my father
had been alive, I doubt I would have shown it to him. After Bobby
died, my parents rarely mentioned him, unless to mark a time or

an event, like using the abbreviations B.C. and A.D. "That was after we lost Bobby," one of them might say. It was an interesting way to speak of his death. He was "lost" to us, it was true. Partially he was "lost" because my parents could not speak about him and when they did, it was always with heaviness and sadness. We lost not only his physical presence, but we also lost the ability to experience together the joy that his presence once brought.

I filed the article away for fifteen years, never imagining that firefight still had the power to change lives.

Chapter 5

Law never made men a whit more just; and by means of their respect for it, even the well-disposed are daily made the agents of injustice.

Henry David Thoreau

Richard Nixon was elected President in 1968 with a "secret plan" to end the war. His secret turned out to be a lot like Lyndon Johnson's: speak about pursuing peace in public, but escalate the war in private. Nixon's private war was at least based on a plan, however covert or ill-advised. Johnson had a tendency to play both ends against the middle and it was the military in the middle.[1]

Grown men argued over the shape of the table for the peace talks. Whether or not they argued over size was less clear. In 1972, Daniel Ellsberg leaked the Pentagon Papers, top-secret documents outlining the deceptions, the ignorance, and the delusions that characterized much of foreign-policy decision-making related to Vietnam. In 1975, the last Marines died in Vietnam during our chaotic, televised exit from Saigon on April 29 and 30, a month after the Americans' exit from Da Nang.

For weeks, the poetry of Howard Nemerov bubbled up at unexpected times, especially when I turned on a faucet. "They say the war is over. But water still / Comes bloody from the taps."[2]

---

1   Peter Braestrup, interview of Lyndon Baines Johnson. Retrieved 21 October 2009 from http://www.lbjlib.utexas.edu/johnson/archives.hom/oralhistory. hom/Braestrup/Braestrup.asp.

2   Howard Nemerov, "Redeployment." *The Collected Poems of Howard Nemerov*, Chicago: University of Chicago Press, 1977.

In 1975, the war in Vietnam ended and a war closer to home escalated, although it was years before I understood the similarities and the connections between the war in Vietnam and the wars being waged in our justice systems. It was years before I understood the ways in which all wars are alike. I rejected the foreign war, but enlisted in the domestic one by becoming a correctional service officer (CSO) for the Arizona Department of Corrections at its Adobe Mountain School for juveniles.

Mom often excused people's excesses by saying, "They mean well," but she also said, "Good intentions pave the road to hell." The juvenile justice system had good intentions. Whereas the adult justice system was openly adversarial, the juvenile system promised a non-adversarial process. Locking kids up was supposed to be for treatment, not punishment. It was all for their own good. A different language was used to reflect the non-adversarial nature of the system. Kids were *adjudicated* instead of convicted. The institution with razor wire coiled around the top of the fences was called a *school*. The kids lived in *cottages*. I was tempted to look for the gingerbread.

The philosophical nuances, however, were lost on the kids. When kids do something and are sent to court for it and then are locked up and have every movement controlled and are fed nasty food and not provided with the conditions they need to flourish, even those of borderline intelligence, of which there are quite a few, tend to see it as punishment. Some of the nuances were lost on us as well. The cottages were named after the military alphabet (Alpha, Bravo, Charlie, and so on), and we used military police radio codes.

After a stint in the security cottage, where kids spent their days locked in cement rooms, I worked in Cottage November, the Girls' Diagnostic Cottage. Incompetent parents were the norm. Of course, I was childless then and thus an expert on the topic. But even so, there were pages and pages that spoke of the worst sorts of neglect and abuse. One mother gave her preschool child heroin to quiet him. He was now a heroin addict. Another mother took her kids shoplifting. The majority of the girls were victims of sexual abuse. Mothers typically sided with the abuser, who was their meal ticket, compounding the sense of betrayal. One father was executed by the state, leaving his son with "anger issues." The son is still doing time.

Some people believed that what these kids needed was discipline. By that, they meant punishment, but these kids had survived about the worst kinds of punishment imaginable. What they really needed were parents who were self-disciplined and accountable. Short of that, they needed a system that was, but they weren't likely to get either.

Parents vacillated between indulgent or neglectful or authoritarian. They gave in to the whims of their children or ignored them when it was easier on them and then, when they couldn't take it any more, came down harshly on them. They likely took rule infractions or even questions as a threat to their authority. They used fear to force compliance. The kids grew up not being able to predict the consequences of their own behavior, which is crazy-making. It also doesn't lend itself to good problem-solving skills. Parents thought they could hold their kids accountable instead of holding themselves accountable. The system took the same approach.

The Department of Corrections had to take whoever the county sent, and counties had a financial incentive to send kids to the state. Any services they offered at the county level came out of their budget. If they sent them to the state, the most expensive option, it was free to the counties. Being sent to the state was like giving people vouchers for fine restaurants instead of food stamps. Kids followed the money instead of the money following the child.

Each county's juvenile justice system operated with great autonomy and also with different resources and philosophies. Kids sent to the state from Pima County, which included Tucson, were usually chronic or violent offenders. The rest of the counties sent a mix of kids, but girls were typically locked up for things that would not get boys locked up. One girl from Navajo County ran away from home, slept with her boyfriend, and shoplifted along the way. One thirteen-year-old from Maricopa County was in for prostitution, and the file noted that her customer, in his fifties, was not charged because he agreed to testify against her. As I locked her door one night, she was squatting on the floor, coloring in a coloring book. What in the hell was I doing?

While kids were in the diagnostic cottage, psychologists ran tests, and we carefully observed their behavior. And then, in spite of their diverse needs, we funneled them into an option: going to a treatment cottage at the institution, going home, or going to a placement in the community. There were fewer placements for girls than there were for boys. Girls who ran away from placements were often not allowed to return, and these girls knew how to run as if their lives depended on it, because sometimes they did.

Whatever their intentions, not all adults had the maturity or mental health to do the job. I later heard about staff members in another cottage who left rooms unlocked to facilitate assaults. Not long before I was hired, a CSO was killed in one of the boys' units. The press demonized the kids involved, calling them "thugs" and worse, but when I got to the institution, some of the staff questioned the CSO's belligerence and his disregard for certain safety precautions. Nurse Ratched from *One Flew Over the Cuckoo's Nest* came to mind. Of course, it is always best to distance oneself in some way from those who end up dead.

Then there was the irony of the keepers and the kept. At one staff training, a tray of drugs was passed around so we could see what the drugs looked like. The tray came back with additional drugs on it, something many found hilarious. Fewer found it funny that some staff and visitors were bringing drugs in for kids. One girl later told me that she had never before or since been able to access heroin so readily. Another, an eighteen-year-old, no longer had bladder control because heroin use had masked the symptoms of venereal disease and left her body ravaged.

"The first time I ever shot heroin was when I was thirteen and locked up in this institution for being a runaway," she confided one night. When it finally dawned on me that a kid I cared a lot about was doing heroin, I went to a staff psychologist and suggested that we do drug tests so we could at least move beyond the denial phase. When he said it was too expensive, I offered to pay and argued that we were putting ourselves at risk of a lawsuit if a kid died of a drug overdose. What I didn't consider was that drug testing would be an admission that we had drugs in the institution. No testing was done.

We weren't just failing the kids, many of whom were victims of the saddest kind; we were failing their victims, past and future. Most of the kids were not particularly dangerous; they were out of control. These kids took most of our energy and resources, leaving the dangerous ones to fly under the radar screen.

Our measure of success was not repairing damage done to victims, whether in the institution or outside the institution. We were looking for compliance in the institution even though there is no evidence that compliant kids or adults are more successful once they are released, and there is *some* evidence that they are less successful, especially those who are in an institution for a long time. Punishment fails to teach new behavior and undermines justice and public safety in other ways. People who are punished tend to see themselves as victims, decreasing any natural empathy they might be able to conjure up for their victims or any connections they might feel to society or the community.

In the midst of all of this, some of us established relationships with kids that were among the most positive they ever had. We anguished over their failures. We loaned them our hope when they lost their own. We had faith in them when they no longer had faith in themselves.

We were devastated when Anita used a pair of borrowed blue jeans to hang herself from the bars over the window in her room.[3] Ironically, only the "security" rooms had bars. Most of the rooms had Lexan windows bolted shut. No one ever got through one of them, so the added security of bars was not needed and only provided an opportunity for suicide that a regular room did not.

When I left the institution, I became a foster parent at the age of twenty-four to one of those girls, Karen, who has remained in my life. I also forged strong relationships with staff members, as our survival depended on one another. But such relationships and such stories did not justify the system. They serve only as examples of how, in the worst of situations, people often find ways to connect and to find meaning. As James Morrow has pointed out, "'There are no atheists in foxholes' isn't an argument against atheism, it's an argument against foxholes."

Whatever our intentions, we were having a hard time winning their hearts and minds, as evidenced by occasional assaults on staff and riots and a revolving door. After a thwarted riot in my cottage one night, I learned there had been a mop handle with my name on it. I drove home in the middle of the night wondering why I would risk my life for the State of Arizona. By staying, was I helping to mediate the abuses or was I helping to perpetuate them? Were my best qualities helping to shape the system or were the worst qualities of the system shaping me?

---

3   Except for Karen, I have changed the names of incarcerated juveniles.

Chapter 6

As one reads history, not in the expurgated editions written for school-boys and passmen, but in the original authorities of each time, one is absolutely sickened, not by the crimes that the wicked have committed, but by the punishments that the good have inflicted; and a community is infinitely more brutalised by the habitual employment of punishment than it is by the occasional occurrence of crime.

Oscar Wilde

I left Adobe Mountain School after fifteen months but went on to work in other parts of the juvenile justice and social services systems. In 1989, twelve years after leaving the institution, I was asked to become the Director of the Governor's Select Commission on Juvenile Corrections.

The Governor's Commission was created as the state's response to a well-deserved class-action lawsuit against the Department of Corrections over inhumane conditions at the Catalina Mountain Juvenile Institution near Tucson. The state initially tried to find experts to testify that the conditions were acceptable, but when that failed, they agreed to separate juvenile corrections from adult corrections and to appoint a Commission to reform the system. The federal court stayed the lawsuit.

I sat on my bed one sunny fall afternoon and began reading the "Proof of Facts," submitted by the plaintiffs to outline their case. Kids were made to rake rocks in extreme heat and were handcuffed to the fence when they refused. Educational programming was barely existent and some teachers were not certified. One teacher lived in his car in the parking lot. In one deposition, the Director of the Department of Corrections, Sam Lewis, couldn't name any differences in conditions between isolation in that juvenile institution and Arizona's death row even though isolation was being used for minor rule infractions and even to keep an eye on suicidal kids. One of the suicidal kids was depressed because he wasn't allowed to attend a family funeral. Because so many kids were trying to hang themselves, the administration decided that staff should wear scissors on their belts.

I walked out into the sun to warm myself and get the images out of my mind. When I finally toured that isolation unit, all the sunshine in Arizona couldn't help. It's trite to say, "I wouldn't treat a dog that way," but those were my first words as I stepped out of the door.

We held public hearings in Phoenix, Flagstaff, and Tucson. The director of a nonprofit program said, "These kids know that what happens to them is not in any way related to what they did." She knew that what happens to kids in the system has much more to do with the whims of individuals, what programs exist and have openings, the amount of funding available (which often was greater at the beginning of the budget year), where they live, their parents' resources, how their parents are perceived by decision-makers, their gender, their race, and a hundred other factors.

The fire chief near the Tucson institution didn't come to the hearing. Instead, he picked up the phone and delivered a brief, but powerful, message: "I sure hope you plan to do something about that place," he said. "My men are tired of going over there and cutting kids down and trying to revive them."

I toured all the institutions. Adobe Mountain was now for boys only. Girls were held next door at a new facility. Buck, the security staff member who cut Anita down, was still there. He took me aside.

"See that kid?" he asked. "He's the kid that Cindy had while she was locked up here." I could see the resemblance and remembered the pregnancy. She wanted an abortion and said that if the baby was a boy, she wouldn't want anything to do with him. Her mother and the judge intervened.

The first thing I tried to figure out was who we had locked up in our juvenile institutions, the end of the line for kids in the juvenile system. The pervasive public perception was that kids were getting away with murder and were just getting their hands slapped for serious offenses, but the most extensive research ever done on kids in our state institutions showed that 15% of the boys and 30% of the girls were being locked up for offenses that would never get an adult locked up. This mirrored numbers in other states. There was only one kid in the system for a first degree felony. Even though all counties still had a financial incentive to send kids to our state institutions, our counties still had different resources and practices and philosophies about which kids to send the state.

There were disturbing, but not surprising, racial disparities. In Maricopa County, kids of color were not being committed to state institutions for less serious offenses than their white counterparts, which surprised some people. They actually had slightly more serious records, but research, like life, hinges on the questions you ask. Upon greater scrutiny, we found that kids of color were much less likely to be given other options or interventions before they were committed to state institutions. After the greater scrutiny, that juvenile chief probation officer no longer spoke to me.

For the first time, I began to see our current practices in a historical context. I learned that I had entered the system just as incarceration rates began to rise in the United States.[1] It was not a coincidence that that was the year the Vietnam War ended.

Nixon first spoke of a war on drugs the year Bobby was killed. This war was not really on drugs, but on poor drug-users and drug-

---

1   In 1975, there were about 300,000 people incarcerated in this country. That number is now at 2.3 million, an increase of more than 600%.

users of color. It was as if we needed an enemy, whether foreign or domestic. And as soon as the Vietnam War ended, we turned our attention to the enemy within. The military no longer served as an alternative to incarceration for young men in trouble. In the absence of a military coming-of-age ritual, doing time became the new marker for manhood among many youth, especially youth of color. Sure, there was a rise in crime and even violent crime, but much of the violent crime was fueled by the war on drugs and incarceration rates are basically an artifact of what we decide to criminalize and what we do with people who break the law. Although poor people and people of color are not more likely to do drugs, they are much more likely to be locked up for drug use.

I'm not big on conspiracy theories, as they usually attribute more planning and intentionality to a system than is deserved. However, if there were a conspiracy to create a system designed to disenfranchise and lock up the most marginalized in our country without garnering too much suspicion, we couldn't have done a better job than our correctional system.

Even some people with power and money wanted no part of it. An Arizona Court of Appeals judge, a Democrat, told me that he and two of his Republican colleagues had a conversation about what country they would pick for their trial if they were charged with a crime, whether or not they were guilty. None chose the United States of America.

Arizona separated juvenile from adult corrections and implemented new legislation aimed at treatment, but, as out-of-state consultant Russ Van Vleet noted, "There has been more harm done to kids in the name of treatment than in the name of punishment." I would hate to have to tally up the harm done in the name of anything, but it does seem that most harm is done in the name of something good. This is true for a country going to war for peace or a parent holding their child's hand over a flame to teach them respect for fire.

The legislation passed in Arizona because we had a lawsuit. We had not changed the hearts and minds of our citizens. In Arizona and in other states, most people's ideas about crime were shaped by the media, and a rise in media attention on juvenile crime was on the way, helping to further skew public perceptions. Those least likely to be victims of crimes reported the greatest fear. They were also most likely to have the power to shape public policy. So the fearful put pressure on legislators to do something, and legislators pandered to the fear and did something. We got tough instead of smart on crime.

We passed laws taking discretion away from judges, who are supposed to be impartial, giving it instead to prosecutors, who are not supposed to be impartial. And it's much easier to observe how judges use their discretion than how prosecutors use it. We passed laws to charge more kids as adults even though we had no evidence that the adult system was well-equipped to even handle adults. We passed budgets favoring incarceration over alternatives. When I asked one judge why he was asking for money for more detention beds instead of much-needed treatment alternatives, he said, "People don't like to pay for alternatives, and programming is the first thing cut when money is in short supply." So we built more bars to hang ourselves and our children on.

Although designed to prepare young men for war, some people thought boot camps were a good idea to prepare young men for more peaceful pursuits, although the research never backed up these claims. The problem was that our boot camps didn't guarantee a job at the end or, most importantly, a place in the tribe, which gangs and the armed services did.

More and more, I felt like a stranger in a strange land. That was about to get worse. Six months after attending my 1990 reunion and reading the details of my brother's death, the headlines read *WAR*. The same policies that failed us at the family, state, and national level were again being used for foreign policy. Although there was little talk of religion in my work in domestic public policy, we always trotted God out for foreign policy. President Bush drew a line in the sand and made it clear he thought that God was on the U.S. side of the line.

And then the press and the policy-makers drew another line, and most people went along with it. Patriots were on one side; people who asked questions were on the other.

Chapter 7

All great social problems involve theological conceptions.

Clarence Skinner

I left the church during the Vietnam War and returned during the first Gulf War. I missed the community that a church can provide, but wasn't sure I could find a place with space for my doubts and my questions. I didn't want my faith questioned if I couldn't, in good conscience (or due to my God-given tendency to ask questions), go along with a certain belief. I also wanted a church willing to ask questions and to stand against injustice.

That first Sunday of the Gulf War, I considered going to a Unitarian Universalist church because I had seen members at social justice events and once heard a respected professor mention being a Unitarian. Even though I didn't like the idea of a church with a litmus test or creedal test for me, I had one for it. If the minister fails to mention the war or just promotes the "God is On Our Side" company line, I wouldn't go back. I didn't go that Sunday, but within weeks I attended Valley Unitarian Universalist Church in Chandler, Arizona.

Both Unitarianism and Universalism were originally Christian denominations that merged in 1961. Most Unitarian Universalists did not consider themselves Christian. Some members didn't even believe in God, and those who did had various images of God.

That God-on-Our-Side God who so often requires human sacrifice was nowhere to be seen. I hadn't really thought about the difference between human images of God and the reality of God. Somehow my literal-minded approach reduced the whole thing down to whether or not God exists based on the image I was taught.

This religion made no claims about knowing that which I believed was unknowable. Instead of an emphasis on life after death, there was an emphasis on life before death. Instead of wondering or arguing about the circumstances of Jesus's birth or what happened after his death, there was an emphasis on how he lived his life. This religion didn't promote the infallibility of any human, especially any human arrogant enough to claim infallible knowledge of God's will. It encouraged me to bring my life experiences and understanding and questions and to look to many sources for wisdom, not just the Bible. Instead of promoting dogma, this religion promoted shared values.

I laughed when one of the writers quoted theologian Reinhold Niebuhr, who said he wanted a religion to afflict the comfortable and comfort the afflicted. That's what I wanted, too. It was a while, however, before I sought the wisdom to tell the difference. I wanted a religion to accept me as I am and challenge me to be better. I didn't know where my religious journey would take me, but this place felt big enough to hold me wherever it took me.

The Sunday of Memorial Day weekend in 1991, I went to church figuring that if the God-on-Our-Side God was going to make an appearance, this would be the time. We sang "This is My Song." It was one of several hymns in the hymnbook sung to the haunting tune "Finlandia."

> This is my song, O God of all the nations,
> A song of peace for lands afar and mine.
> This is my home, the country where my heart is,
> Here are my hopes, my dreams, my holy shrine;

But other hearts in other lands are beating
With hopes and dreams as true and high as mine.

My country's skies are bluer than the ocean,
And sunlight beams on clover leaf and pine,
But other lands have sunlight too, and clover,
And skies are everywhere as blue as mine.
O hear my song, thou God of all the nations,
A song of peace for their land and for mine.[1]

Here was an image of a God big enough to love the whole world and not just a piece of it. The Rev. Jim Norman was in the pulpit. He began by bringing out his Marine Corps sword still in its scabbard. I had one just like it in my closet. Although he had been in the Marines in the 1960s, he hadn't gone to Vietnam, which left him feeling relieved, sad, and guilty.

I was home.

War drove me from church, and it hastened my return. Within weeks, I could speak to others what I knew after my first visit. I wanted to enter the Unitarian Universalist ministry.

I waited five years to begin seminary, but immediately my thinking about the justice system began to shift, and so did my thinking about religion. Why do we fail to use what we know and what research tells us? What is the source of resistance to well-thought-out public policy? It seemed to come down to that fundamental human need for *us* and *them*. The irony of our need to see some as *other* is that it is this need that actually fuels anti-social behavior all the way around. It creates the very resistance that we say we are trying to overcome. And I was quite effective at creating resistance. I had a different *them* than they did, but I still saw myself in pitched battle against those who didn't get it.

Why do we live within the guidelines and laws and rules created by social institutions? Mostly it is a sense of connection.

---

1   Lloyd Stone, "This Is My Song." Lorenz Publishing Company, 1934.

It is a sense of not wanting to disappoint or to be shunned or to be judged harshly by those who matter to us. It is a desire to belong to the tribe. This allows us to live together in community and to promote a greater good, and it allows us to be manipulated for narrow interests and for nefarious purposes. It is why our institutions and culture must both promote and protect our sense of connectedness while valuing dissent and varying viewpoints as part of what makes the community stronger. Without this, there is no accountability and no safeguard against abuse. Healthy systems always allow people to ask, "Why?"

I rejected fear-based, authoritarian religion after my brother died and then went to work in a system based on that brand of religion. I began to see that there is religion that divides and religion that unites. One approach is to separate the saved from the unsaved, the saint from the sinner, the heretic from the believer, the infidel from the faithful, the sheep from the goats. Salvation is an individual affair. The other approach emphasizes the unity of all life and the interdependence of life. We are all in this together, and we are saved or lost together. In the early twentieth century, Universalist Clarence Skinner wrote that the line between good and evil runs through people, not between them. That's still a radical idea.

Religions that divide often rely on fear for compliance and equate faith with believing the right things. Those that unite see fear, rather than disbelief, as the opposite of faith. These different approaches exist within most of the world's religious traditions so that there is greater difference within each major tradition than between them.

A religion that divides, a religion that worships a vengeful God, sees retribution and punishment as integral to human justice. I was sexually assaulted in my early twenties and understood a desire for sure and swift vengeance. Soon that desire for vengeance transformed into a desire to understand why someone would be that sick. I wanted him, whoever he was, to understand what he did and take responsibility for it. I wanted to make sure he never hurt someone else. I wanted a justice system to build on my best hopes, not pander to my worst fears and impulses.

And that's the type of religion I wanted as well. I didn't want a justice system that relied on punishment any more than I wanted a religion that relied on threats of hell. A fear of hell or a fear of jail doesn't keep most people on the straight and narrow. Maybe that's because most people who believe in hell or in jail mostly believe in them for other people.

I found the religion I sought and, not long after, I found the new philosophy of justice. In 1990, Howard Zehr, a Mennonite, published a book called *Changing Lenses: A New Focus for Crime and Justice*. Retributive justice focuses primarily on the offender and on rules and asks: *What law was broken? Who is to blame? What is the punishment?* Restorative justice takes the victim and accountability seriously and asks: *What are the hurts? What needs to be done to repair those hurts? Who is responsible?*

Chapter 8

Perhaps the whole root of our trouble, the human trouble, is that we will sacrifice all the beauty of our lives, will imprison ourselves in totems, taboos, crosses, blood sacrifices, steeples, mosques, races, armies, flags, nations, in order to deny the fact of death, which is the only fact we have.

James Baldwin

In the summer of 2001, I spent two weeks in Ireland. On the island of Inis Mor, we visited a memorial for fishermen lost at sea. When it was being planned, the people on the island gathered to remember the names that belonged on the memorial, and they still remembered names from a hundred years before. What would happen if people in Boulder City gathered to remember war dead, I wondered. Who would remember Bobby?

The Irish speak of "thin places" where the veils between the worlds are thin, and we can glimpse other realities. I began to think of times of crisis and loss as thin times, when new things become possible out of our own understanding of what we control and what we do not control. I was living in a thin time.

My mother had suffered a stroke and heart attack sometime in the early morning hours of Mother's Day in 1999 and died three days later. In the summer of 2000, my husband and I divorced. In November, 2000, my good friend and mentor Mike Garvey had died of a heart attack just days after telling me, "I live vicariously through you now." Lucile, that arbiter of good taste when Bobby died, was also gone, having lived long enough for me to understand her demons and learn to love her. Other relatives were gone, too. My son Luke was having serious trouble navigating his way into adulthood. Thin times. There was so much I didn't control.

And in 2000 and 2001, I had completed four hundred hours of hospital chaplaincy. I was assigned to the Pediatric Unit, the Pediatric Intensive Care Unit, the Neonatal Intensive Care Unit, and the Oncology Unit at one hospital, and I rotated occasionally to Arizona's busiest Level One trauma center to work sixteen-hour shifts responding to all codes and in-coming traumas. On one shift, there were twenty-three.

The first patient I visited was a new mother unexpectedly facing a heart transplant. The first dead baby I saw was named Luke. Less than an hour later, I saw my second dead baby. The faith of some people comforted them; the faith of others afflicted them. Some expected comfort from their faith and were pleased or disturbed based on whether or not they got it. Others didn't expect comfort, they expected strength. They expected to have their hearts opened and to learn something important, and they were rarely disappointed.

In my own life and in my work in the justice system, I saw the power of suffering to close the human heart. *You hurt me. I will not be hurt again. You hurt me. I will now hurt you.* Here, not for the first time, but in new and starkly intimate ways, I watched the power of suffering to both close and to open the human heart, even in the same hospital room. In the presence of a dying child, one heart opened to the suffering of every child and another heart closed in anger and blame. Neither was necessarily permanent. How was it with my heart? What in my heart closed with each death? What opened?

In the fall of 2001, I headed to the Pacific School of Religion in Berkeley with another member of my church and good friend Terry Sims. On the morning of September 11, 2001, as I was rising, my friend Margi called and told me to turn on my television. Word soon spread through the dorm, and though Terry and I had our own televisions, it was a time to be with others.

Even in my own grief, I worried about the opening and closing of hearts in my country. Just like in hospital rooms during my chaplaincy, I was seeing both. Would we build new bars to hang ourselves and the world on?

The next day, Terry and I went to see the Vietnamese Zen Buddhist monk Thich Nhat Hanh, who sought to be open to all the suffering during the Vietnam War and emphasized that the means and the ends cannot be separated, that to take sides is to deny one-half of reality. As a result, his publications were considered threatening to both the North and the South, and he went into exile in 1966. He spoke softly. The bell rang. He spoke softly. The bell rang. He spoke softly. The bell rang. My eyelids grew heavy. I was awake enough to know that the point was to carry that oasis of calm with me into the world where there was already talk of retribution. Individually and collectively, we have trouble staying in the pain. We want to move immediately to the anger. And so there is more pain.

I had left the church during war. I had returned to the church during another war. The drumbeats of war sounded as I searched for my first congregation. In 2003, less than two months after my ordination into ministry and my formal installation as minister at the Unitarian Universalist Church of Ventura, California, we were again at war.

In the fall of 2002, as a new minister, I began a tradition of offering up a sermon topic for the church auction. A young man in the congregation paid over three hundred dollars and asked for a sermon on sacrifice. We chose a Sunday during the annual pledge drive, but that week we went to war and so I looked at this new war through the lens of sacrifice.

Typically we define sacrifice as giving something up, but the root meaning of the word refers instead to "making sacred." What were we being asked to give up and what were we making sacred in this call to war? As usual, some were being asked to give all. But with no draft in place, my son was safe as long as he didn't volunteer. The noble act in life is when we give up the reality of our comfort and safety for the lives of others or to affirm life, not when we give up the lives of others for our comfort and an illusion of safety. I was asked to sanctify my own comfort in the form of the American way of life and the illusion of Homeland Security. This is why it was easy for me to support the noble impulse which motivates most of our troops and yet oppose the often ignoble impulses of our foreign policy. And that's what I preached about that first Sunday after the war began.

In December, 2003, I learned that my sister was dying of brain cancer. Although she always spoke openly about the death of others, she was not talking about her own death, and she was aggravated at people who already seemed to have her buried. She wrote me that she didn't plan to die soon "or maybe ever."

The first anniversary of the war in Iraq passed. My sister was dying, whether she liked it or not, and the anniversary of my brother's death was on Easter.

My childhood theological take on Easter was that God sent his son to die for our sins. Jesus probably could have come down from the cross using supernatural powers, but he showed tremendous will power by refusing to do so. Jesus knew that this was not really the end, though. At least, he was pretty sure. And he was able to forgive those who killed him. And then, after he died, he literally came back to life again, and we can, too, if we have faith and believe in him. This is still how many Christians relate the story.

My mother was never all that religious and certainly not steeped in the finer nuances of Christian doctrine. A few years before her death, she said, "I could never figure out why someone would like the idea of a God who sent his son to die for someone else's sins."

"Well, Mom, not all Christians believe in that interpretation. Some don't even believe that Jesus was literally resurrected," I answered, but her eyes glazed over.

Leave No Brother Behind

Many Jewish and Christian theologians tell us that we must wrestle with the old stories to discover how they speak to us today. As I struggled with the story, here is how it spoke to me on the anniversary of my brother's death. Jesus didn't die *for* our sins. Jesus died *as a result of* our sins, and he died brutally. People who were threatened by him decided that to nail him to a cross was the best way to eliminate the threat. Although it is convenient to be able to say that it was God's will, it's wrong because it makes God a scapegoat, too.

For some, the belief in a literal resurrection is of central importance. For me, the belief that his body was literally resurrected and that he knew that this would happen dilutes the power of the story. As the German Christian theologian Dorothee Soelle has written, "No heaven can rectify Auschwitz."[1] Indeed, no heaven can rectify crucifixion. No heaven can rectify war. What if Jesus remained loving and forgiving because he knew that affirming love in the face of hatred and life in the face of death and evil is the only ethical stance? What if Jesus *couldn't* come down from the cross using some supernatural power, but *could* face his death and his suffering because he knew that his message would live on, because he knew that no empire can wipe out the revolutionary message of love, no matter how oppressive the regime or how violent its means?

The Easter affirmation that *The Lord is risen today* affirms that the message of love remains and the power of love lives on. Can we, in the face of death, affirm life? Can we, in the face of hatred, affirm love? Can we, in the face of hopelessness, affirm hope? Can we, in the midst of suffering, affirm joy? The Easter story tells us that we can.

We are given both life and death. We are given both love and hatred. We are given both greed and generosity. Were we not given

---

1   Dorothee Soelle, *Suffering*. Minneapolis, MN, Fortress Press, 1975.

both, choosing would be meaningless. We often want to skip Good Friday and go straight to Easter. Until we recognize and understand the power of death, we cannot truly affirm and choose life. Affirming life is not the same as denying death. Recognizing the power of death, we choose life.

When we give into cynicism and despair, we let suffering and death have the final word. Every death is a promise unfulfilled in some way. It is up to us to fulfill the promise. Jesus told his followers what that meant to him. *Go love one another as I have loved you. That's how you will keep me alive.* That's it. That's enough. And that message has survived in spite of all efforts to water it down or pervert it.

There are many things we should be able to expect from religion. And one thing is that it should strengthen us. It should show us that as long as there is life and love, there is meaning and hope. It should show us that love is available to us in every moment. It should help us affirm life in the face of death.

I preach what I need to hear and that's what I preached on that Easter in 2004, on the anniversary of my brother's death while my country was at war and my sister was dying. By Easter of 2005, the crucifixion and resurrection story would say something new again.

PART II
The Search

Chapter 9

History is merely a list of surprises.
It can only prepare us to be surprised yet again.

Kurt Vonnegut

In February, 2005, Luke sent me one of his rare emails. I could hear his deep voice as I read the entire message: "Check this out." There was a link to a website.

I knew immediately that it was about my brother, but this was not like two guys at the door. This was not Dad at the bottom of the driveway. I didn't know that my world was shifting.

On the website, there were two brief postings.

16 Oct 2001

Chris,

I might forget you, but I kinda doubt it. Your namesake lives on. Rest in peace, old friend.

Semper Fi,
Bill Ager

5 July 2002

I am proud to have served with Lieutenant Christian. He was a fine officer and a good man. What a loss, as were all our loses [sic]. Lieutenant Christian signed the adoption papers for my two daughters, he is now and will always be missed.

Lance Corporal Marvin R. Thomason

I sent emails to both guys, marked the virtualwall.org website, and then forgot about it. Weeks passed. One Friday night, I came across the bookmark again and realized I hadn't heard back from either guy. Bill had listed a phone number in Virginia. The next morning, on March 5, I dialed the number. It was disconnected, but I found another listing in a nearby town and a woman answered.

"Hi. I'm Jan Christian and I'm looking for the Bill Ager who was in Vietnam with my brother, Robert M. Christian, Jr."

"Oh. . . . Well that might be Bill. What did you say your brother's name was?"

"Robert M. Christian, Jr."

A pause. "Well, yes." Another pause. "That may be my husband."

The conversation continued for a few minutes, and then she said, "You are going to think that the first part of our conversation was really strange given what I am about to tell you, but I was just in shock. We have a son named Robert Christian Ager. Bill has been looking for your brother's family for thirty years. He even contacted the high school in Boulder City. I was just working on my lessons for a Sunday school class I teach. This is a miracle."

When I told my friend Margi about the call, she asked, "Don't take this wrong, but why would he name a son after your brother? Did your brother save his life?"

"I doubt it. Bobby was just an amazing guy. One of his high school friends, Richard Corderman, had twin boys before Bobby's death, and one was Bob and the other was Chris. There was a guy Bobby knew at Quantico who told us that if he ever had a son, he would name him after Bobby."

But after I spoke with Bill himself the next afternoon, I was less sure of my explanation and didn't really have one to offer in its place. Bill said they met at the Cao Do Bridge. He didn't remember a lot of specifics. He remembered playing cards with Bobby and that Bobby wanted to get a sail boat. He remembered my brother as being "irreverent, cocky, and bright." That was sure true. He heard that Bobby sent an outpost out one night but lost contact with them and went out himself to bring them back, which Bill called "extremely dangerous."

In April, Bobby and his guys were in an area known as Dodge City in what was called the Arizona Territory. On April 5, the whole battalion moved out on foot. There were multiple firefights and casualties within Lima and India Companies. On April 7, Kilo Company was sent out alone, and they set up a combat base and were there Monday through Thursday digging up bodies and food caches and whatever they could find. They were harassed by the enemy every night. Bobby had been leading 1st Platoon, but he had 2nd Platoon for this operation.

On Friday, at daylight, Bobby went out. Bill heard on the radio that he was down, so 2nd Lt. Tom O'Connor (whom Stephen Gregory had referred to as Petersen in his article about that day) was sent out. When they realized Tom was also hit, Bill and everyone else went out, and they called in an air strike. It was around lunch time, and they were out of water and low on ammo.

The next day, Bill went to Da Nang to identify Bobby's body. Another Marine was there to identify Johnnie Lee Anderson's body. Bill stopped by the hospital to visit Tom O'Connor. Tom was a lean, handsome guy. When the nurse led Bill to Tom's bed, he thought there must be some mistake, as Tom's face was swollen beyond recognition.

"So what was it about Bobby that made you name a son after him?" I asked.

"Chris was just squared away. He was doing an impossible job and doing it well. I sure didn't do it that well. Not long after that I was working in the rear," he answered.

This was not really what I expected.

"Basically those guys needed a big brother. Chris was a big brother to them," he added.

"Well," I choked out, "Bobby had a lot of experience at being a great big brother."

I told him about my big brother. Unlike most officers, Bobby joined because he was drafted. He supported himself through college, working full-time and earning a double major bachelor's degree in four years. Upon graduation, he lost his student deferment and was drafted. Instead of waiting around for six weeks to be inducted, he decided the sooner he went in, the sooner he would get out. He joined the Marines on June 29, 1967. I didn't tell Bill that I was staying with an aunt in Birmingham, Alabama, when I heard the news, and that I had cried myself to sleep on her couch that night.

I told him about the poem Bobby wrote and that I heard he called my dad and told him he wanted out while he was at Quantico. Bill said, "Well, we knew how the war was going to end by early 1969, but we were right to be there. Our cause was noble. Someday, Vietnam will no longer be a communist country, and your brother's death will have played a part in that."

"I don't believe that," I said. "I tried for a while to believe that he died for a worthy cause, but nothing I have ever read has allowed me to believe that. I don't think we had any business being there. I think his death was a waste."

Bill was sorry to hear that my father, mother, and sister were all gone and that he had missed the chance to talk to them. "I always regretted not writing your family right away. My regret really increased when my first child was born in 1973. I wrote a letter in 1979 that got returned and then I made contact with a nurse/ midwife from Boulder City in 2003 and I thought she was going to help me, but nothing ever came of it. I found out that one of my daughters even hired a private detective at one point. I posted to every website I could find."

"If you had contacted us right away, it would have been nice and soon forgotten. You would have told us what we already knew.

The fact that you have searched for us all these years makes it that much more of a gift, and the fact that you are in touch with me when the rest of my family is gone makes it all that more poignant for me," I said.

His son was there and Bill put him on the phone. Robert Christian Ager said, "I got a call yesterday from my mother and she was kind of crying, and I was scared because I thought something was wrong and then she told me about your call."

The next day I awoke with the heaviness of that first grief deep in my bones. Tears came to my unopened eyes. I was both disturbed and comforted because my grief reconnected me to my brother as well as to my father and mother and sister. I remembered a time when letting go of my grief over my brother's death seemed disloyal because it meant severing some important connection to him. I missed him and he was back. They were all back.

But in the days that followed, I realized my connection was more to my grief than to my brother. I couldn't conjure him up. I could remember the voices of my father, mother, and sister, but not Bobby's. I remembered images and sentences and phrases, but I wanted to remember how he moved and the sound of his laughter. My grief this time was focused not only on losing him, but on losing the details of his life. How had I let that happen? Was this the price for getting on with my life?

I sent Bill a copy of the article by Gregory and a copy of the condolence letter we received from 1st Lt. Tom Hobbs. I wrote that I hoped his contact with me was not disappointing or troubling, because, unlike me, he had decades of expectations, and I had shared a very different view of my brother and his death with him.

He wrote back:

There was nothing disappointing or troubling in the things you shared with us on the phone. We are just so very glad that you contacted us and shared with us so many things about Bobby and your family. You took a big chance contacting us because you really didn't know what to expect. You are brave, just like Bobby. Yes, we are different in some ways, but share many more things in common. We already love and accept you and are very happy that you seem to feel the same way toward us.

That Easter I preached: "Out of the Ashes . . . Life Again."

We Unitarian Universalists say that our good news is that "we need not think alike to love alike." Bill was living that out with me. And with his love and acceptance, it came to me in a flash. There is something important that I have never forgotten and will never forget about my brother. The little details may have faded away, but I will always remember what it felt like to be in his presence: safe, loved, honored.

Jan and Bobby Christian

Jan and Bobby Christian

Chapter 10

Man . . . cannot learn to forget, but hangs on the past:
however far or fast he runs, that chain runs with him.

Friedrich Nietzsche

*O*ur family spent a lot of time on Lake Mead. Our first boat was
christened with my nickname, Tan Tico, which was my way of
pronouncing *Jan Christian*. In my last overnight there with my dad
and brother, I provided the entertainment by planting my right
foot on the shore with my left foot still on the boat. The boat began
to drift ever-so-slowly so there was plenty of time to watch as I
achieved something akin to the splits and then fell into the water.
And then there was the water dish that I brought for my apricot
poodle, Chamois.

"A water dish for a dog? At the lake?" Guffaws were followed
by intermittent chuckles and head shakes.

I was never drawn to roughing it; it was all about the water
for me.

One summer we were out in the middle of the lake with my
first foster sister Annie, who kept asking, "Are we in the middle
of the ocean?" The vastness of the water was something to behold.
My dad killed the inboard/outboard motor and announced that
we were going swimming.

"How deep is it?" I asked.

"About five hundred feet," he estimated.

"I can't swim in water that is five hundred feet deep."

Dad's response was, "What's the difference between five feet and five hundred if you can't touch the bottom in either one?"

I stared into the water. One difference was that I couldn't even *see* the bottom here. What was down there was a total and utter mystery. Whether my faith was in my father to save me or in the ability of the water to support me or in my own ability to float or tread water, I do not know. Maybe I just didn't want to risk his disappointment. I jumped.

The strange thing about water and faith is that, if you break faith, you are likely to sink. Fear causes you to sink like a stone. You might be able to flail around for a while to keep yourself from drowning, but eventually you are going down. Floating is only possible if you trust the water and can surrender to it. Surrender in this case is not giving up, but giving oneself over to something capable of holding you. Faith, in this case, is the opposite of fear. I learned that lesson early with water, but applying it to life is a different matter.

I didn't think much about what was at the bottom of my investigation into Bobby's death when I started out. A few people, including my ex-husband, Michael Roach, questioned my pursuit and advised caution. He had enlisted in the Marines at seventeen and did two tours in Vietnam. I didn't think of myself as naïve, but he asked more than once, "Are you sure you want to do this?" Sometimes he added, "Some things are better left alone." When I said that I was sure, he always added, "Be careful."

On March 22, I talked to Marvin Thomason, the second person who posted on the website. He hadn't answered my email from weeks before, but he had an email address with a company name in it so I searched for that company and found his name and work number and left him a message over the weekend.

When he called back, his first words were: "Your brother saved my life." Marvin, who went to Vietnam in 1968, was married to a woman who had two daughters, ages three and five. When the adoption papers arrived, Bobby witnessed them and then, recognizing Marvin's family responsibilities, arranged for him to go to school in Okinawa. While Marvin was away, his best friend, who was Stephen Thomas Hall, Bobby, and the man who replaced Marvin were all killed.

The phone connection wasn't great. The wind was blowing across his cell phone. He had stepped outside to talk to me.

"I got abuse as soon as I got into the Los Angeles airport," he said. He was the first of many to speak of the poor treatment received upon returning from Vietnam.

"Some things are better left alone," he concluded. I understood. It was my last conversation with him.

Even Bill Ager mentioned that it was "brave" of me to contact him. Bravery is when you feel fear and do it anyway. I didn't have a strong sense of risk. What was I missing?

Some things should just stay buried. This seems to be one of those accepted pieces of wisdom, but how do we know if this is true? Some buried things are like bodies buried near the water supply. We keep drinking from the well and wondering why our life is poisoned. Sometimes what we think is buried is really keeping us from the life we long to live, and we may not even know it. Sometimes we sense it but think the answer is to bury the body deeper. There are other times when life here and now really is good and there seems to be no real need to muck around in the past, and yet, the past may help us see the larger tapestry that is our life and reveal and deepen connections.

For many years after my brother's death, my father had nightmares. Once he grabbed my mom's arm in his sleep and left it bruised and sore.

"What are you fighting in your sleep, Dad?" I asked.

"Oh, lions and tigers and bears. I'm not afraid of anything," he said, and we laughed.

When my father was a young man, he and my mother met a man who knew my father's family. "Oh, I remember your father," he said to my dad. "He's the one who committed suicide."

My father was only four when his father died, and this is how he learned of a family secret. Years later, I tried to show my father a photograph taken of me and another staff member and three of the girls at Adobe Mountain School. I pointed out Anita and said, "She's the one who committed suicide."

"I don't look at ghosts," he said, pushing the picture away.

In the weeks before his death from cancer, he was often confused. As his defenses were lowered and he faced death, I wondered if he might talk about Bobby. He didn't, but an event from his childhood haunted his dreams and he awoke one night deeply disturbed.

"Remember when we were in Cullman and they burned the blacks out?" he asked my mother.

"I wasn't there, but you told me about it a long time ago," she said. When he was a little boy, growing up in Alabama, some uncles took him to Cullman, Alabama, where blacks had been brought in to help work on the railroad. When their work was over, the shacks the railroad had provided for them to live in were burned, and they were told to leave.

"I should have killed those men," he said about the men who set the fires. It was entirely possible that he was referring to his own relatives.

When my mom told me this story, I remembered another told by a family friend years earlier. Dad was riding the rails as a teenager. As part of a crack-down on stowaways, railroad workers were told not to rescue people who got trapped in cars. My dad inadvertently got himself into a refrigerator car and was in danger of freezing to death. When the train stopped, he put his mouth up to the drain pipe and yelled for help, although he knew that, even if someone heard him, they may not respond. A black porter opened the door and saved his life.

70

In the last week of his life, he had hallucinations. As I was growing up, one of his favorite expressions was, "I wish I'd been a cowboy." In one of the hallucinations, he was on the side of the Indians, fighting other cowboys. How had the experiences of my dad's boyhood shaped his life? I doubt that even he knew the answer to that.

I wanted to know more. I wanted to know how the events of my childhood were still playing themselves out in my life. Questions about my brother's death and his life that I had not known to ask or had not dared to ask before now surfaced. Was my brother really such an extraordinary person? Why is it that some lives touch us more than others? Surely, the circumstances of his death and the age at which he died made it all more poignant, but wasn't it really more than that? How did his life shape my life? Was his death still shaping my life? Why did he choose the Marines? Didn't he know better? *What was he thinking?* What caused a man who didn't know him all that well to name a son after him? What really happened that day? Were there other guys who remembered that firefight or my brother? Were there other keepers of the memory out there? Who were these guys who were with my brother in the last few months of his life and in death? How were their lives changed by their experiences?

I was transported back to that time, but things were different. Now I brought with me years of experience. Might these allow me to see some things that I could not see before? I was in the strange position of being able to look at the life and death of my older brother from the perspective of being much older than he was when he died. Would some of my earlier perceptions hold up under closer, wiser scrutiny? What if they didn't? And how could they? I had rejected all things military even to the point of ignoring the military connection on Memorial Day weekend worship services, and now I was reaching out to former Marines?

We often speak of "closure." If people speak of the past, even in the spirit of learning more about it, we often say they are living in the past. Might they just be finding new ways to let the past live in them? We sometimes speak positively about confronting the past, which speaks of the past as enemy. Might we not befriend the past or make peace with it instead?

We build our images of ourselves on our understanding and interpretations of the past. If we change our understanding of the past, something in us must change, and often that something is our core identity. Maybe it is this fear of being changed that keeps us from going back. We know that going back will change the way we go forward.

Going back into my past would also mean going back into the nation's past in a culture where mucking around in the past or even knowing about the past is not all that valued. Most Americans prefer to think that we wake up to a new world every day only to create the present out of brand new material. We often have no idea of how the past lives in us and shapes each day. In my reading about Vietnam in the 1970s, I was shocked at our policy-makers' lack of interest in or appreciation for the history of Vietnam and its people.

I hadn't sought out these contacts. I wasn't feeling a need to confront my past or even make peace with it, but here it was, and I knew it had something to teach me if I let it. Going back can change the way we go forward. I knew that it would not always be easy and that I would have to go to places I had never been. I would have to look at ghosts.

I jumped.

Chapter 11

Where'er we tread 'tis haunted, holy ground.

Lord Byron

I t's one thing to jump; it's another to push someone else, but I did
that, too. I found Tom Hobbs through an unofficial 3rd Battalion, 1st Marine Division (3/1) website. I knew his name from the
letter he sent us in 1969. He responded to my email immediately:
"I remember Bob and the date as I've relived the day on numerous
occasions."

Tom retired as a Colonel and was working in recruiting at
Marine Military Academy in Harlingen, Texas, where I reached
him by phone. Right away he told me that Bobby had strong character and loved the responsibility. Every morning a patrol went
out to clear the area. Bobby convinced Tom, who was only slightly
older, to send him out that morning. Bobby had been a Platoon
Commander in Kilo Company, one of four rifle companies in
Third Battalion, First Marines. Having done his time in the bush,
he was transferred to the Weapon's Company, but he missed the
action of a rifle platoon.

"I've thought a lot about letting him talk me into sending him
out that morning," Tom said.

Bobby took his platoon out, and Hobbs could hear the firefight.
There was no radio contact so he sent Tom O'Connor's platoon

to see what was going on. Tom was hit. The officers were using PRC 6 and PRC 9 (pronounced "Prick") equipment, which was fairly new and probably not a good idea because it helped identify leaders to the snipers.

Hobbs was nearby when Tom O'Connor and Bobby were evacuated, and he believed they were both killed in action or "KIA." Hobbs continued. "It wasn't until three or four days later that I learned that Tom had survived. We had four KIAs and many WIAs that day and about seventy enemy KIA." I knew that there had been only two Marines killed that day and that Bill Ager visited Tom O'Connor in the hospital the next day.

Tom Hobbs and his wife were planning a recruiting trip to Woodland Hills, which is less than an hour from my home, so we arranged to meet there in a month.

My next conversation was with 2ⁿᵈ Lt. Tom O'Connor, who was shot in the face that day. This is the guy Gregory mistakenly referred to as Peterson in his article. Tom later said, "Yeah, my fifteen minutes of fame and he gets the name wrong."

Tom began, as most of the men did, by saying he was sorry for my loss.

"I'm sorry for your loss, too." I didn't know the impact of his wound, but I figured it must have been serious.

O'Connor was a Boston College graduate and older than Bobby or "Bwob" as he calls him with his thick Boston accent. He joined the Marine Corps in his junior year and then went right to Officer Candidate School upon graduation. He joined Kilo Company on the same day Bobby did: December 21, 1968.

"I was really glad to see him that day," he said.

"You knew him already?" That hadn't occurred to me.

"Well, I didn't really know him but I knew of him. We graduated TBS (The Basic School at Quantico) together in November, and he stood out because he was so intelligent. There was another guy who stood out, too, because he was a gung ho Naval Academy grad. I don't know if you would recognize his name or not. He was

Oliver North."

"Oh, yeah, I recognize the name." *Oliver North and my brother were classmates?*

"Well, when I saw Bob, I thought, 'They are teaming up the dummy with the smart guy.' My strong suit was my athleticism. His strong suit was intelligence. In fact, I didn't know what to call it then, but I've since learned the expression 'thinking outside the box.' That's what Bob did. He was always out front and took charge of any situation. He was being groomed to be the company commander."

"I heard that while Bobby was at Quantico, he called my dad and told him he wanted out. Does that surprise you?"

"No, like I said, he was intelligent."

I liked this guy immediately. He was self-effacing and a straight-shooter. My brother would have laughed and rolled his eyes at my choice of words.

"Bob was always writing letters. He had a map in the rear with pins in it, and he told me he had given his parents a map so they could see where he was. I thought, 'That was smart. Why didn't I think of that?'"

I told him about my conversation with Marvin Thomason and Bobby's efforts to get him to Okinawa.

"Now that's just what I'm talking about. I am trying to hustle little plastic wrappers to put on the maps and your brother is pulling strings to get someone to Okinawa."

He began with lighter memories. "Some of our time over there wasn't all that bad. We started out in the First Tanks area which was pretty easy. Later we spent time at the Cao Do Bridge which wasn't too bad. Bob and Tom Hobbs were on the north side and I was on the south side. They got the penthouse. I got the outhouse."

"Where were you when you raided the whore houses?" I asked.

"Oh," he laughed. "Did Bob tell you about that? That was when we were at First Tanks. They sent us in by helicopter and made a big deal of it," he said with disgust.

"The action on April eleventh really started on April fifth. It was a Battalion-sized operation with three rifle companies. This was Dodge City in the Arizona Territory in the An Hoa Basin, south of Da Nang. It was a major enemy encampment. On the fifth, there were numerous Marine casualties including two lieutenants, Steve Donaldson and Butch Geary. Two days later, Kilo Company was sent out by itself. We had a gunnery sergeant at the time who, talking about the Battalion Commander, said, 'That SOB is sending a Company out to do what he couldn't get done with a Battalion.' Kilo Company was right in the enemy's positions and their bunkers. It was like being behind enemy lines during World War II. Our job was to dig up graves to estimate enemy dead from April fifth, so we could justify the casualties that day."

O'Connor confirmed that, in this Vietnamese war, there was really no front. To a certain extent, our guys were always in enemy territory but not always literally on top of the enemy. Since it was not about taking territory, the body count was important. We called it "a war of attrition." When we couldn't win hearts and minds, we settled for bodies.

When I read him some of the Gregory article, he said it was exaggerated. "We were well dug in at night although we did have activity the night before and took some casualties," he said. "Each morning it was our routine to sweep the area, and Bob took out two squads to do that. I was asleep, but we could hear the firefight and they lost radio contact and so Lt. Hobbs sent me out to see what was going on. I remember going out there, but I've lost about fifteen minutes of time."

Tom agreed with what Hobbs had said about the PRC 6 and PRC 9. "There was an antenna on the helmet and the transmitter would go in a pocket or in the flak jacket. They might as well have given us targets to wear."

One of Tom O'Connor's brothers was in the Army in Vietnam

at the same time and came to visit a few weeks before Tom was hit. He met Bobby, who took a few pictures of the O'Connor brothers.

"When my brother came to visit me at Bethesda Naval Hospital, the first question he asked me was, 'How is your friend, Bob? How did he make out?' Recently there was a Battalion reunion and people were allowed to get up and talk about someone they wanted to remember. I got a tape of it, and I was playing it while my brother was around. There was this 1st Sergeant who got up. I can't remember his name, because we just called him 'Top.' He got up and started speaking, and my brother said, 'Hey, that's your friend Bob he is talking about.' That's how he always says it: 'Your friend, Bob.' When other guys start talking about him, I think, 'Hey, he was *my* friend.'"

Tom O'Connor has two sisters and two brothers. One brother went to Canada to play hockey and stayed there. Tom lives in a house in Cambridge that once belonged to his aunt. He worked in accounting for twenty years but was never very computer savvy. He began working in residential construction but was injured two years ago (his "second worst day") and his counselor now thinks he should be retrained in accounting.

"What were your injuries from Vietnam like?" I asked.

"The bullet went in under my right eye and came out under my left ear. I have permanent paralysis on the left side of my face with Bell's Palsy-like effects. I lost hearing in my left ear, and three months ago I had surgery on my left eye trying to save some vision in it. I go to the VA three to four times a month. When people see where the bullet went in, they tell me I'm lucky."

"You don't think so?"

"If I was lucky, it would have missed me. Basically, it was a day that didn't have to happen," he said.

"I think it was a war that didn't have to happen," I said.

"When we talk about April eleventh, we say, 'That is the day we lost Lt. Christian.'"

April eleventh is the day Tom O'Connor got shot in the face and he remembers it as the day we lost Lt. Christian?

We arranged to meet in May when I would be in Boston on business. I sent him the Gregory article and a link to my sister's article about my brother, which included his poem. My sister emphasized my brother's gentleness and that he was not raised for war. Tom wrote back, "Thank you for the picture and website. I'm sure I will be reading the article and poem over and over as I have already. In Robert's poem, the four young men would be reference to a fire team, (there were) three fire teams to a squad." He concluded, "All that pain because of the chance meeting of two opposing sides. April 11 was our fate, but I like Robert was not raised for it, God will have to explain that day to me sometime."

Tom sent a picture of my brother with Les Levy and two other guys and wrote, "Les has a funny story to tell you about the picture."

In June of 1968, Les Levy was a 2nd Lt. at the age of twenty-two. When he became the Executive Officer (XO) for Kilo Company, he handed over 1st Platoon to Bobby, who came in wearing a white t-shirt. Les let him know that white t-shirts didn't cut it in the bush, and he swapped t-shirts with him. The picture shows Les in the white t-shirt, Bobby in the green t-shirt, and two younger Marines, Danny Gallagher and Buck Albright. Of the four, only Les survived. Danny Gallagher, holding his beer in a glass mug and smiling broadly for the camera, was killed shortly after the photo, on January 21, 1969. Buck Albright died on May 23, 1969. I later learned of my own connection to Buck.

"I have a vivid image of everyone who died," Les said. "I can see Bob just like it was yesterday. I was on my second R&R on April eleventh. When I got back and heard, I just sat down. I was just devastated. To this day, I have carried guilt thinking maybe if I had been there." His tears came first and I loved him for them.

I always asked the guys about their lives since Vietnam. Les, who had graduated from West Virginia University, lives and works in Orlando with his wife, whom he married over three decades ago. His mother, a Holocaust survivor, lives in the Boston area. When he returned from Vietnam and considered going back, she talked him out of it.

Les mentioned a Harvard graduate named Peter Waldinger who was their Forward Observer (FO), but hadn't been located since.

"How hard could it be to find a Harvard graduate named Peter Waldinger?" I asked.

I sent Les the Gregory article, and he wrote back about his return from Vietnam and his search for healing. "I moved to Boston when I got out of the Marine Corps, but left a year later in 1971 because of the liberal attitude and anti-war sentiment that prevailed." He got tired of "being ridiculed" for serving his country and "being called a 'baby killer' and all the rest of the rhetoric of the time." He put everything he owned in his VW, "moved to Miami, bought a sailboat, and sailed around Florida and the Bahamas for a year."

"It was," he wrote, "the best thing I could have done for myself and my head." I could picture my brother doing the same thing. He and a friend built sailboats in our driveway from kits, and his dream was to buy a sailboat and sail around the world.

"This is a humbling and moving journey I am on," I wrote to Les. "Remembering can be an act of bravery and everyone I have contacted has been willing to do just that."

Another veteran lived in Mesa, Arizona, just next to Tempe, where I lived for almost thirty years. I might have passed him on the street without knowing he was the man who knew my brother's last words.

Rick Miles was born in Ohio and joined the Marines at age eighteen. He went to Vietnam in December, 1968, and was mostly with 1st Platoon, Charlie Squad. Rick got out in 1976 and married Sandra in 1979. They have four children and three grandchildren. After saying that he was sorry for my loss, Rick made a statement that is repeated in novels and memoirs about the war.

"There were two kinds of officers," he said. "One would stand up and fight with you and would put his men first. The other kind would send others out, but try to keep themselves safe. Your brother was the first kind. I can give you an example of the second kind. There was a second lieutenant who sent out a listening post. That was four men. They were supposed to go out a thousand meters but they only went out a few hundred and they got hit by our own mortars. They started yelling and the lieutenant said it was a trick and wouldn't let guys go get them. We had to hold him at bay with a weapon so we could go get them and two were dead. That would never have happened with Lt. Christian because he made it a point to know his men and all the details about them before he ever went out with them. I want you to know that I had the utmost respect for your brother. We always felt a lot safer with him. I know that your brother saved men that day and so did Anderson. I didn't see it, but I think Anderson knew he was dying and that he intentionally rolled onto that grenade," he said.

I was not prepared for his next statement.

"I remember your brother's last words," he said.

In the split second between that statement and his next, I knew that I would not stop him. Of course, I did not want to know and, of course, I had to know.

"Your brother's last words were 'What's going on? What's happening?'"

My heart sank. My brother, who was always sure, always calm, always positive, spent his last moments like this?

"Do you think he was expecting an answer?" I choked out.

"No, I think he was trying to answer it himself. He was just trying to stay alive," he answered.

Rick went on to fight on No Name Island on June 7, 1969, and he called in an air strike, "but it was already over." Eight Marines died. One of them was Donald Arribi who was wounded the day my brother was killed.

"I got a call from a woman a while back who wanted to know the details of Anderson's death. When I told her, she just broke down and cried," he said.

"Was it his sister?" I asked.

"I don't remember who she was," he answered.

But I knew. Johnnie Lee Anderson had a sister, too. And I would find her.

L to R: Danny Gallagher, Les Levy, Buck Albright, Bob Christian

Chapter 12

The tragedy of war is that it uses man's best to do man's worst.

Henry Fosdick

Before we met in person, Tom Hobbs told me to look for a 6' 4" guy wearing a yellow polo shirt with "a high and tight haircut. Once a Marine always a Marine." Tom retired from the military and his initial conversation with me was fairly formal so I expected something along the lines of "Your brother was a great guy. You should be proud. He died doing something important. God speed," but I couldn't have been more wrong.

Tom and Jane were in the lobby sitting side by side with their eyes focused on the front door so they were already starting to rise when I saw them. She is petite, with short hair and warm eyes. This is a couple that can still turn heads.

We made our way to the restaurant and they sat beside one another and I sat across from Tom. The yellow polo shirt had a red Marine Military Academy insignia. Of course, the Marine colors. I ordered a sandwich and they ordered Cobb salads.

"How did the two of you meet?" I asked Jane.

"I was a flight attendant based in San Francisco. We met in 1969 right after Tom got back from Vietnam."

I began to comment on the longevity of the relationship, but she continued.

"And today will be the first time I have ever heard him talk about Vietnam. His mother said he came back a changed person. I didn't know the other Tom. I think Tom has always been emotionally repressed." Tom didn't respond.

What I had done began to sink in. I pushed Tom into the water. The waiter quickly got the idea that something important was happening and interrupted only when necessary. When the lunch service was over, he said they were having a staff meeting nearby but that we were welcome to stay.

Tom had told me that he had relived the day many times, and that is what he did that day. It was as if he was watching a fast-paced movie that only he could see. His narration came in snatches, and sentences were incomplete, but Jane and I got the picture.

During lapses in his narrative, Jane and I spoke, but Tom was mostly silent. I ate half of my sandwich. Jane barely touched her salad, but Tom ate every bite of his. *Bless your heart,* I thought. *You are a Marine.*

"I heard it all began on April fifth when the entire Battalion went out and sustained quite a few casualties," I said.

At first, Tom said he didn't really remember that, but later he said, "There was a machine gunner who wouldn't go forward that day. He knew we were getting into some bad stuff. We got him out of there fast because we didn't want it to spread."

"You were out there digging up bodies to justify the deaths on the fifth?" I asked.

"Body counts were important, but I'm not sure what we were doing out there. I know there were extensive underground tunnels that had probably been there since the French. There was an ROK[1] compound in the area that had apparently not been doing much of anything. I read later that was for political reasons. We also had reports that there was a blond man, believed to be a deserter, in that area, but we never found him."

---

1   Republic of Korea.

Tom asked for a piece of paper and drew a primitive map. He stared at it as if seeing the actual territory. He tapped his finger on it several times, trying to get control of his emotions. Jane and I held our breaths.

"They said 'Let's send a company in there and see if it can survive.'"

Jane and I looked at each other with tears in our eyes.

"You could put me down in Da Nang and I could find the exact place. It might be under water, but I doubt it. It might be developed, but I doubt it. I could find it," he said, still staring at the map.

"Have you ever thought about going back?" I asked.

"Yes, I have thought about going back and taking my sons."

I said, "Maybe I will take my son and we will go back together."

He nodded.

I asked a question that had been on my mind since our first conversation. "You said before that Bobby talked you into letting him take his platoon out. Was the sweep going to happen anyway and it was just a matter of who went out?"

"Yes. We made a sweep every morning." he answered.

"So someone was going to go out that day?"

"Yes."

If my brother talked him into sending him, then it must have been someone else's turn? I didn't ask.

Tom looked at the map again. He knew Bobby was hit so he sent Tom O'Connor to see what was going on. In my previous conversation with him, I got the impression that they had just lost contact, and he wasn't sure what had happened. Tom was adamant that Johnnie Lee Anderson was black. I later learned that a Jimmie Lee Forrest was killed on April fifth by a short round (a bomb dropped too soon). That might be the death he was remembering, because Johnnie Lee was white. Collapsing two traumatic events into one is not unusual.

"I remember the tank coming through with Tom and Bob's bodies on it. Both bodies were on the same side of the tank. I saw blood on their heads. I didn't go over any closer. I thought they were both dead." He repeated this several times during our conversation.

"I've talked to Tom O'Connor," I said. They were both curious. He and Jane asked a number of questions: Do you know if he ever married? How is he? What is he doing?

"I sent my aunt to visit Tom when he was in the hospital in Bethesda." Tom said.

"That was nice," I said.

"I called your folks when I got back to San Francisco. I talked to your mom. 'What happened to my boy…..what did….how?' I was going to visit, but it never happened." He trailed off. It was as if he was holding the phone in his hand.

"That must have been a really hard call. I can understand why you never visited." I pictured a young Tom at a pay phone, my mother hysterical on the other end. The idea of crawling in a spider hole looking for Viet Cong might have been less scary than visiting our house after that.

"Most of what Gregory wrote was highly exaggerated," Tom said. "No wounded human being could carry all the ammunition that he said he was carrying and do what he did." But Tom did speak of the desire for revenge and his efforts to keep things from getting out of control in the days that followed. The air strike and ROK troops leveled everything later that day. Later on, some guys took an enemy they had killed and strung him up like he was crucified "probably in retaliation for that day."

Jane talked about their sons. The older son, a lawyer, is married and lives in Austin. The younger son traveled to Vietnam and other countries, staying out of touch for months at a time. He is a vegetarian and not interested in material things.

I thought, "Oh, how the universe seems to give us children who can teach us everything we need to know about ourselves." But I said, "Gee, I bet there have been some interesting father/

son dynamics in your house." Jane nodded. Tom expressed concern about teaching his son responsibility, but some of the dynamics have Jane rethinking their priorities and values. I told her I could relate to that.

"My son went through a really rough patch," I said. "He went into a great wilderness program which was transformational for his dad and me. One of the staff from the Anasazi program said to us, 'The sign of a good parent is not how your child turns out, but your ability to be loving and responsive in every moment.' I knew I was not in control of Luke and yet I didn't realized how much my desire to be in control of him was creating resistance and showing a lack of faith in him. I try to remember to have faith in him and let him know that."

"I think it would be really good if I told my son that. I feel like you have been sent here to tell us these things," she said.

And later she asked, "Do you worry about your son being drafted?"

"Yes, but I think if we are going to have a military there should be a draft. I don't think our military is as 'voluntary' as we like to think," I answered. She nodded.

"I do think that young men need to find out what they are made of, but I think we need a better way than war to help them find out." I added.

"I think they get that at the prep school where I work," Tom said. "Some good things came out of the Vietnam experience for me, but I would never want that for my sons."

We began to talk about books and films about Vietnam. "Have you seen *Fog of War*, the film about Robert McNamara?" I asked.

"No, but I remember his plan to send a hundred thousand of the most expendable kids," Tom answered.

"I think they call that 'ethnic cleansing,'" Jane said. I found myself liking them both more all the time.

"Well, McNamara still doesn't get it, as far as I'm concerned. He is evidence that intelligence alone will never save us," I said.

"I think the best non-fiction book about the war is Sheehan's *A Bright Shining Lie*,"Tom said.

I agreed. An ambitious and sweeping work, it gave chilling details about the captivity of a young man from my home town, Doug Ramsey, a civilian who was taken prisoner in 1966 and not released until 1973. Dan Ellsberg met his plane. Doug's parents went to our church. In my senior year of high school, his dad used to come into the drug store and sit at the counter where I hung out drinking cherry limeades while my friend Denise worked. I don't ever remember a full-blown conversation with him, but there were a few precious times we made him laugh.

"And *Fields of Fire* did the best job of showing the chaos and confusion of the war,"Tom added.

"It sure did. One thing that I've taken from most of my reading is just how chaotic things could be," I said. "It's one of the reasons that I am so surprised that guys remember April eleventh and can distinguish it from other days. I would think that everything would just flow together for the most part."

"That day stood out. I sure have relived that day many times. I still feel guilty about it," he said. We all had tears in our eyes.

"Tom, you were young. You were in an impossible situation. You were doing the best you could," I said.

Not all of Tom's memories were painful. "I remember a Battalion Commander who traveled with a two-hole shitter. During one firefight it was blown up and word quickly spread among the entire battalion that it was not enemy fire that blew it up. So some guys were never recognized for their good deeds there that day." We laughed.

Towards the end of the conversation, I again raised the idea of going to Vietnam. Tom said it would take some serious planning.

"What do you think?" I asked Jane.

"Oh, I don't know. I would have to think about whether or not I would go."

"What about for Tom?"

"I think it would probably be a good idea. I will have to think about it. I will have to see how the rest of the day goes. Tom really agonized over this meeting and this conversation and I was very apprehensive about it." Tom seemed to flinch at the word "agonized" but did not deny it.

"I knew my past would eventually catch up with me," he said.

What had I asked of him? Everything. And he did what all of his training prepared him to do. He did what he believed was the right thing whatever the cost to himself. He faced the past by sitting down with the sister of a fallen Marine brother and looking her in the face. So often the greatest acts of bravery go totally unheralded or even noticed. I wondered what the ramifications of this act of bravery would be in his life and in their life together.

After four hours, I left the hotel dazed, feeling almost feverish. It wasn't due to anything I learned about my brother or the day he died. It was due to understanding more deeply how that one firefight on one day in one war changed lives and was changing them still.

Back on the 101 freeway headed home, my cell phone rang with a message. It had gone straight to voicemail. It was Tom thanking me for the visit and telling me that he and Jane would be back in late July and hoped to see me then. Relief washed over me, but it was almost two years before I heard Tom's voice again. It was not until I, too, had walked in the Arizona Territory of Vietnam.

Chapter 13

The life of the dead is placed in the memory of the living.

Marcus Tullius Cicero

On the morning of May 18, 2005, I took a short walk from where I was staying on Beacon Hill to the Frog Pond in Boston Common to meet Tom O'Connor. As he approached, he held out a Filene's bag with the words "Something Exciting Always Happening" written on it. Inside was a box of truffles. This simple gesture moved me then and moves me still.

We walked to the Public Gardens. When we came to the footbridge over the pond, he pointed out a plaque. "I just found this recently on the internet," he said. It was a tribute to 2nd Lt. Michael P. Quinn, a Marine killed in action on August 29, 1969, who worked on the swan boats in his teens. The boats are so named because the figure of a swan partially covers the paddleboat captain at the rear of the boat. My eyes took in the tranquil scene.

Tom pointed to a nearby area fenced off to allow privacy for two swans that have nested together for years. "We used to call them Romeo and Juliet. It turns out they are Juliet and Juliet!" he said.

"How appropriate given that Massachusetts recently approved same sex marriages," I replied.

"Are we on the cutting edge or taking a few steps backwards?" he asked.

"I think you're on the cutting edge. What do you think?"

"What do I know? I'm a member of the 'Walking Dead Society.'"

"How so?" I asked.

"I read the expression in a book. It was used to describe wives who never got on with their lives after their husbands died in war. But on the marriage rights thing, I say, 'Live and let live.'"

We walked to an indoor food court, a place he comes often. Although he lives in Cambridge, he often spends Sundays at the Common. We got our food and headed to an area with mostly empty tables, where we sat for hours.

Tom's parents came to Boston from Ireland as young adults. Tom is the only one of their five children who hasn't gone back to Ireland to visit. There were nuns on his mother's side of the family and four priests on his father's side, one of whom started a Catholic church in Woodland Hills, where I met Tom Hobbs. Tom's dad worked for forty-seven years as a room service waiter at the Parker House.

"I guess you know that Ho Chi Minh once worked at the Parker House?" I asked. We smiled at the irony of that.

"Bob and I never thought we had an April eleventh in our future," he said. I wondered if this was true for Bobby. Could you really go to war and not have a sense that you might die? Well, I guess the evidence was all around me. People go to lawyers to write a will "in case something happens," as if death is only a possibility. Men in battle often seem to either have a strong sense of the inevitability of their death or a sense of immortality. Others figure it's a crap shoot.

"I'm not crying," Tom explained after another swipe at his face. "This left eye just waters. The surgery I just had was to tighten it to help keep it from watering and it has helped." He pointed to the tiny spot under his right eye where the bullet entered. "They tell me the guy who took care of me must have been an artist, but I've found out that bullets usually do more damage coming out than going in."

He pointed to his left ear and the indentation under it where the bullet exited. He has no hearing in that ear. When he speaks, it is out of the right side of his mouth. A young woman at the VA Hospital has been working on his teeth. "It's part of her master's project. She wants me to have my jaw broken and reset, but after all these years . . ." He shrugged and his voice trailed off.

Since I am in Boston twice a year on business, this was the first of many visits with Tom O'Connor. Success and failure are common themes. Success is defined as a long marriage, a good job, and a family—things that have eluded him. Unlike many people who are disappointed, Tom not only marvels, but revels, in the successes of others. He remembers the exact details of successes in the lives of others and counts them and describes them as easily and as reverentially as one might count beads on a rosary.

One of the guys told me, "Tom O'Connor was one gung-ho son of a bug." Tom doesn't describe himself that way, although he admits to a sense of competition in the bush.

"If Bob took a night patrol out one night, I took one out the next night," he said.

Those days are gone. He will go along with a "hoo-ah" every now and then but gung-ho expressions and macho posturing seem mostly to amuse him. After an email made the rounds condemning the surrender of some British troops in Iraq, Tom said, "Yeah, it's easy to be brave sitting behind a desk." He gave his half smile and chuckled. He is not going to judge people harshly who are in impossible circumstances.

The next day we got together with Pete Waldinger. After Les Levy mentioned Pete, Tom and I set out to find him. My internet search eventually came up with an article from Skidmore College about a class of '68 alumni volunteer named Jeanne Waldinger. At the end of the article, it listed her email address and her husband's name: Peter. In the meantime, Tom walked over to the Harvard alumni office and asked if he could get an address for Pete. They weren't allowed to give out addresses, but offered to forward a letter. Pete, who had not been in contact with anyone from the Marine Corps since leaving the Corps, received Tom's letter, my email and another letter from a classmate at The Basic School within a few weeks.

I arrived at Emmet's Pub on Beacon Street early, took the round table at the window, and ordered a Guinness. Pete, a thin man about 5'7" with a confident demeanor and a ball cap that read "Marine Corps Scholarship Fund" walked in about ten minutes later.

Pete is a retired investment banker still married to the woman he became engaged to the day before his discharge from the Marine Corps. They live in Dover in the house Pete grew up in. "It's been my legal address since 1950," he said.

"Dover is a very exclusive area west of Boston," Tom told me.

"And Tom lives in the People's Republic of Cambridge," Pete replied.

"It can't get too radical for me," I said.

Pete went to prep school and did a lot of sailing as a kid. "I led a very sheltered childhood," he said.

"Why did you join the Marines?" I asked.

"It seemed like a good idea at the time," he responded. I laughed, remembering only then that this was a favorite expression of my brother's. Pete went to Quantico in February, 1968, and to Vietnam in October, 1968. Lewis Burwell Puller, Jr., the son of General Lewis "Chesty" Puller, the most decorated Marine in the history of the Marine Corps, was in his class. I had read Lew Puller, Jr.'s book, *Fortunate Son*, in which he chronicled his struggles after losing both legs and most of his hands in a landmine explosion. Although the book had an upbeat ending, his life did not. He committed suicide in 1994.

Pete was a candidate for pilot's school, but the test was on the day after the death of a good friend, and Pete walked out without completing it.

I filled Pete in on some of my findings and contacts. "I've met with Tom Hobbs and his wife, Jane, plus I've had phone and/or email contact with Lou Buell, Jim Crocket, David Crawley, Les Levy, Rick Miles, Steve Rentch, Ken Roysden, Doc Seguer, Jack Stubbs and Marv Thomason."

"She has a stack of material this big," Tom added, holding his thumb and forefinger a few inches apart.

"How long have you been doing this?" Pete asked.

"Since March."

"Of this year?" His jaw dropped.

"Yes, less than two months," I answered.

Tom wanted to credit me with finding Pete, but I reminded him that we both found Pete.

Pete let me know early in the conversation that he is vague about names and faces. "I just never was good at that. I remember your brother and the day Bob died, but no details," he said. And then the conversation turned to hockey. He and Tom remembered every play and every player.

Later, I asked Pete what he remembers. "I don't remember what the date was, but I remember that day. It was a bad day. It was the worst day in Vietnam."

"What made it the worst day?"

"Well, we lost two lieutenants and some others—Bob and another lieutenant." I pointed to Tom with a questioning look on my face.

"Yes," Pete replied. "I thought Tom was killed in action that day and I believe I put Anderson's body on the chopper."

"I don't even remember who went out first that day, whether it was Bob or Tom, but I remember that after the second one was down, we all went in and I called in air support. I left Kilo Company a week later, but I wrote my dad and asked him to go visit Tom when Tom got back to Boston from Bethesda Naval Hospital, but my dad died of a heart attack before Tom made it back to Boston," he said.

"How old was your dad?" I asked.

"Fifty-four."

"My ex-husband's dad died while he was in Vietnam, too. He was forty-four," I said.

"The Marine Corps and Red Cross were amazing. Within thirty-six hours I was back," he said.

"I have always wondered how it must be to be home or on R&R and then have to go back."

"I didn't really think about it. I just did what I had to do," he said.

"I have heard that there was some controversy about an award for Johnnie Lee Anderson based on whether or not he accidentally or intentionally rolled over on the grenade," I said.

"I was told he rolled on it intentionally and thought it was worthy of Medal of Honor consideration, but no one asked me," he answered.

As we walked out of the restaurant, I thought about how weird this must have been for Pete. His expression was often one of someone trying to figure out how two pieces fit together. I had mentioned that I come to Boston twice a year for my work, and he surprised me by saying, "I'll see you in November." That was when I could still be surprised by the depths of these new connections. It was before I could have imagined that at Pete's first Kilo Company reunion, in 2008, I would hold him tight, willing him on as he walked ever-so-slowly past all of the names on The Wall.

And so began our semi-annual gathering in Boston, which expanded to include others. Les Levy was at our next gathering in November and again on my brother's birthday on May 15, 2008. Both Pete and Les brought their wives to that dinner.

On my first visit with Les, we spent two hours at Panificio on Charles Street before the short walk to the Frog Pond, an ice-skating rink at that time of the year, to meet the others. Tom O'Connor, who falls off the radar screen at times, was late. I called his cell phone and left a message.

"Tom, I have your home address and we will show up on your door step if we have to," I said. He walked up ten minutes later.

"Who's walking point?" Les asked. Tom and I volunteered and led the way to Emmet's, where we sat for four hours. Pete went home after our meeting the previous May and told his wife what Tom Hobbs's wife said about Tom never talking about Vietnam. He was surprised when Jeanne answered, "Well, you never have either."

I teased Pete about telling me that his memory was not that good and then remembering every hockey play from decades ago. He nodded. Pete's memory has been jogged by our time together and by some old letters. He remembers losing forty-three pounds in thirty-three days in An Hoa. He wrote his parents at their home address, but the more pointed letters he sent to his dad at work.

"I read some of those letters to my dad recently," he said. "I'm sure they didn't cause my dad's heart attack but it crossed my mind that they may have been a contributing factor."

On my visit in May, 2006, Pete and Tom and I were joined by Glenn Keith, who is married with two sons and works for Clarks Shoes. Unlike Tom and Pete, Glenn was an enlisted man. He grew up in New Hampshire and was commuting to Boston at age eighteen to work a job he hated. He knew it was just a matter of time before he got drafted. One night he and his father got into an argument and the next day he joined the Marines.

The day after that first visit in Boston, I flew to Atlanta to spend time with cousins before heading home. I had the aisle seat. The middle seat was empty, and a young man in uniform was in the window seat. He kept unfolding and reading his orders. I took a look and saw the part about "NO ALCOHOL." That ruled out buying him a drink.

"Where are you headed?" I asked.

"I've been home two weeks and I'm headed back to Iraq," he answered.

"I was just with a Vietnam veteran yesterday, and I asked him how it was for him to be home on leave and then have to go back. How is it for you?" I asked.

"I think it's harder to go back. I sort of wish I hadn't been back here, although it was good to see my kids." He was silent for a few moments. "I don't want to go back," he added.

"And I don't want you to go back."

What else was there to say?

Tom O'Conner had sent me the video from a former reunion in which Sgt. James Crockett stood up during the memorial service to speak of my brother. Jim had pulled a piece of paper out of his pocket and spoke of the thirty-seven "fine Kilo Company Marines" killed during his tour of duty. But Bobby stood out. "I loved this man. I would like for you to think of him as I do," he said.

Jim was living in Powder Springs, Georgia, right next to Marietta where I was staying in a hotel with other relatives in town for a family gathering. He met me in the hotel lobby and we took a table in the breakfast area.

"Bobby was one of the finest young men I've met. I make contributions to the 1st Marine Division in his name. I was in Hawaii for five days on R&R when he was killed. When I got back and was told, it just tore me up. I asked what he was doing on patrol. Bob was always asking for advice. He was always trying to learn. Before I left on R&R, he talked to me about getting a chance to go to the rear and he wondered if he should take it. I said, 'By all means. You've done your time in the bush.'"

Jim retired from the Marine Corps in 1981 after thirty years of service, which included time in Korea. Up to that point, he had been to every reunion. His wife died of a heart attack in the elevator of their hotel at one reunion.

I had come to a conclusion about my brother that I had not spoken before. It was hard for me to speak it without crying. My voice caught in my throat.

"It is clear to me that my brother had many opportunities to take himself out of harm's way, but he did not," I said.

"No, it would not have been like Bob to take himself out of harm's way," he responded immediately.

We walked out to the parking lot and hugged. When he got to his car, he turned and said, "You head on now. I don't want you to see me cry."

L to R: Tom O'Connor, Glenn Keith, and Pete Waldinger at Emmet's Pub

Chapter 14

What has been plaited cannot be unplaited
—Only the strands grow richer with each loss.

May Sarton

There was another sister out there. Ever since Rick Miles mentioned hearing from a woman who asked about Johnnie Lee, I figured Johnnie Lee had a sister and, if she was out there and asking questions, I wanted to find her.

Through my internet research, I knew that I could order a copy of the letter President Nixon sent to the family, and that it would give me Johnnie Lee's home address and his father's name. When the letter arrived, I found that his parents were addressed as Mr. and Mrs. Hobert Anderson at an address in St. Paul. This was good news. Even though the last name was common, the first name was unusual, at least where I come from. I looked up phone listings around the country for Hobert Andersons. There weren't any in Minnesota, but I found one in Troy, Michigan. I realized that a call from me could be shocking so I began by saying that I was looking for a Hobert Anderson who used to live in St. Paul. The Hobert Andersons in Michigan had no connection to St. Paul.

I called a Hobert Anderson in North Carolina, and the woman who answered said they were from Minnesota. I knew I had found Johnnie Lee's family.

"I'm looking for the family of Johnnie Lee Anderson who was killed in Vietnam." I said.

"That's not us," she answered. "We lived in St. Paul when our son, Larry, went to Vietnam, but he came home."

It crossed my mind that she might be suffering from dementia. What were the chances of a coincidence like that?

There are so many times in life when we take the most complicated route when a simple one would get the job done. All of my contacts began because of a webpage paying tribute to my brother, and that is the way I eventually found Bonnie Anderson. She had posted a message on a webpage paying tribute to her brother, and once I found the website, I found Bonnie and her email address.

I emailed her, but weeks passed before she wrote back that she wanted to talk to me because John "was supposed to get the Medal of Honor and never did." I sent her my phone number, but it wasn't until April 5, 2006, that she wrote, "I know it's been a long time since your last email. I recently got a note from a young man in Rome, Italy. He had read about John and contacted me. He referred to an article written by Stephen Gregory. I got a copy of it from Rick Miles. It certainly was a gruesome account of my brother's death. If it would be OK, I would like to call you. Some things I guess need closure and this is one thing that I need to finally deal with." She called me on April ninth, just a few days short of the 37th anniversary of our brothers' deaths.

Bonnie was living in Vail when John was killed, but she happened to be visiting home and had even fielded a call from John shortly before from Australia, where he was on R&R. She could tell he had been drinking, but he seemed more at peace than he had been.

"John had some problems before he went over, and when he first got there, he was saying that he just wanted to kill himself some gooks. He was carrying around the severed ear of a Vietnamese. His early letters were really graphic, but then he started questioning what he was doing over there," she said.

"When the Marines came to the door, I was comforting a friend whose boyfriend had just died in a car accident. We suspected it was suicide. He was a Vietnam veteran and when he got back he slept with a machete under his bed. My younger brother was home, but our parents were three hours away at our lake house. The Marines went up there to notify them. How they managed to drive home, I will never know."

"I don't suppose his body was viewable," I said.

"My dad was friends with the funeral director, and he insisted on seeing John's body. He took to drinking a lot after that," she said.

"What about the funeral?" I asked.

"A friend of John's just went goofy and tried to rip the flag off the casket. Her breakdown lasted for months. I don't know whatever happened to her."

"What about other members of your family?" I asked.

"My younger brother just fell apart. He was on tranquilizers for a few weeks and then he wanted to join the Marines even though he was only seventeen. Basically, he wanted revenge. My dad had been in the Marines and he was proud when John joined, but he pulled some strings so that my younger brother never made it to Vietnam. My brother later had a son who was born on the anniversary of the day John's body came home, and he's named after John. I think that put a burden on the kid."

"How is your brother doing now?" I asked.

"I haven't seen him in years. My dad died in the seventies, and my mom died about ten years ago. She died a bitter woman, and she and my brother were estranged when she died."

"Oh, Bonnie, that is so sad," I said, thinking of the different ways we lose people and wondering how much John's death had to do with the other losses.

"After John died, I just tried to ignore it all," she said. "It all came back for me with Kerry running for President. I went to see a traveling version of The Wall in Ft. Myers. I was having trouble figuring out where John's name was. Two guys just appeared and put their arms around me and walked me over and talked to me for a long time. I just bawled and bawled. They were like two angels."

Chapter 15

For peace we need more than the moral equivalent of war;
we need an intensity equivalent of combat.

William Hocking

On April 30, 2006, I was driving back from Las Vegas where a friend and colleague, Anne Hines, and I had attended Unitarian Universalist District Assembly. We were about twenty-five miles out of Las Vegas when traffic slowed. There was a small boy lying on the side of the road, perfectly still. A Ford Explorer was on its side about fifty feet away. We pulled over. We left the conference early to beat the rush out of Las Vegas and the late Sunday afternoon traffic in the LA area. I didn't have medical training and neither did Anne. What could we do? We got out.

The rest of the family was still in the van and others were working to get them out. I picked up something resembling a shower rod and handed it to the rescuers who used it for leverage to get in a window. A young boy came out, completely covered in blood.

"Come over here and lie down," I said, guiding him away from the van. He shook his head.

"My sister is dead," he replied.

"Come here. Come lie down," I took his arm and insisted.

It was twenty minutes or more before the California Highway Patrol arrived, and later still when the emergency medical team arrived. But just as two ministers happened to be passing by, so did two family practice physicians, some nurses, an ER doc and his former EMT wife. The ER doc called out what we had when the EMTs arrived.

"Twelve-year old girl dead on the scene," he reported.

Maria, the mother, and Heidi, the older sister, flinched. I walked up to him and said, "If you need to do that again, would you not say it so loud?"

"Oh." He looked around. "Sure."

Later, he came over and apologized and asked what my medical training was.

"Actually, I'm a minister," I replied.

He looked around and my eyes followed his.

"That may be better," he said, but I didn't even want to think of what it would have been like to come across that scene without medical personnel.

It was midday and about ninety degrees. Other cars stopped briefly and occupants handed over something we might need before heading off: blankets, an umbrella, a flat of bottled water. One young woman seemed grateful when I gave her a bag and asked her to gather the family's belongings which were strewn all over. A utility bill here. A dress shoe there.

For ninety minutes, Anne and I did what we could just to be there with Maria, the mother, fifteen year-old Heidi, and Danny, as paramedics and volunteers assisted them and four year-old Peter, who had a skull fracture. Someone had removed Danny's blood-saturated clothes, so he was only in his underwear. The blood must have been the older sister's, Luvia's. Others stood over him, but I kneeled next to him and moved my fingers up and down his bony arm. He was the calmest and most present of the family members. He asked about the others so I told him about each member of his family and the plans to get them to the hospital.

"What about Luvia?" he asked.

"I haven't seen her yet." It was literally true. His sister's body was still in the van, covered by a dress, but we both knew the truth.

Maria made phone calls in Spanish and kept trying to tell Heidi that Luvia was dead.

"I don't want to hear it, Mom!" Heidi answered.

Finally the adrenalin surge that had kept Maria upright subsided. She lay down next to Heidi and began to moan. Her condition declined and the plans to take Maria and Heidi by ambulance were changed to take them by helicopter. Heidi began to protest. That is something she could not, would not do. No way.

Anne and I had both had conversations with them, but, at this point, something shifted. Instead of just trying to be a comforting presence, I looked into Heidi's eyes.

"This is bad. Really bad. This is scary, I know. And you can do it. You *will* do it. I have faith in you," I said.

She looked directly into my eyes for the first time. And she did it.

When the family was evacuated, three by helicopter and one by ground, the only volunteers left were the ER doc and his former EMT wife, along with Anne and me. We sat side by side on the side of the road. We talked about what we had seen and what we had done. Mostly we just sat sharing an intimacy beyond words.

For days after I returned, I kept checking the Las Vegas Review Journal obituaries on-line to see if Peter made it. I left a message for the family at the mortuary. The images kept coming back to me. I couldn't shake it. It was like a chipped tooth that my tongue couldn't stay away from it. Yep, there it is. There it is again. The world I came back to was unreal. Why was I sitting in meetings discussing mundane things when people were dying by the side of the road? Memories and images from my hospital chaplaincy returned. A father brought to his knees by news of his daughter's death. Holding a teenage girl so she didn't slip off the gurney while a chest tube was inserted. Bones sticking out of skin. And dead babies. Lots of dead babies. The scuffed up bedroom slippers on a mother's feet and the way her feet fell to the outside when she understood, through the translator, that her baby was dead. A mother touching each eye lash of her dead baby. A father dipping his finger in the baptismal water in a tiny seashell and then touching the water on the forehead of his dead son. A nurse hanging a towel over the window in a room to give the family privacy.

Early in one eighteen-hour shift, a toddler was killed in her own driveway, run over by the family car when a slightly older sibling knocked the car into gear. For hours, wave after wave of family members showed up at the hospital only to learn the ghastly news. If I had gone home afterwards, I would have had a good cry. Instead the next trauma came, and I went to the long trough-like sink in the trauma room to wash my hands. I was hypnotized by the water. Were these really my hands? As the water fell over them, I thought of the Robert Frost line: "And they, since they were not the ones dead, turned to their affairs."[1] By the time I got home, I was beyond tears. I got out a piece of paper and red water-color paint and dropped the paint onto the paper like so many drops of blood.

I can stand to see anything.

Nothing can touch me.

But here's a greater truth. There was something I didn't want to shake. In those moments, the social constructs that separate "us" from "them" fall away. Age, race, religion, class, culture, gender, education. Those things mean nothing. We are one. We understand that we share a common humanity that trumps all of those false boundaries. We are joining with others in a struggle. We do what we think we cannot do. Our own preferences and petty concerns fall away. We are part of something greater. There are connections made in those moments that are true and strong and beyond explanation. Perhaps it is more accurate to say that the connections

---

1   Robert Frost, "Out Out." *The Complete Poems of Robert Frost*, 1916.

that are always there are simply *revealed* in those moments, and we get to glimpse how things really are.

Some of my life's most gratifying and transcendent moments have been moments of connection with people not like me. Times when, in spite of our obvious differences, we have found our common humanity. Joseph Campbell wrote that it isn't meaning we seek, but the experience of being truly alive. And in the midst of death, in the connection with others, I have felt truly alive. These moments became the heart of the chaplaincy experience for me. I lived for the vibration of the pager, the Code Blue call. I understood the expression *adrenaline junkie* as well as I understood *shell-shocked*.

Although it is nothing like the war experience, it's the closest my experience comes to those of the men from Kilo Company who are seeking one another and finding one another after all these years. There were bonds forged in that time that none will ever forget and that many will never again approximate. They were in it together. They depended on one another. That is what motivated my brother. It was the intimacy of a shared struggle, of a common language and purpose.

Down the road, Anne and I stopped for a drink at a fast food restaurant filled with Mexican families partaking in what appeared to be their weekly ritual. I looked at them in a new way. I know you, I thought, and I'm glad we are here together and not by the side of the road. Perhaps my look conveyed what I was feeling: We belong to one another. A teenage boy and I exchanged smiles. Real, crinkly-eyed smiles.

Two years later, Maria came across that message I left at the mortuary and called me. Her words poured out. Peter lost half of his brain. He tries to walk. He can't see out of one eye. Luvia was a good girl. She used to rub her mother's feet. She always went to school but the week before the trip she told Maria she wanted to stay home from school. "I told her, 'OK mija' and we went for manicures. She wanted to pay because my birthday had been on April sixth. I think she knew something was going to happen." They had been on their way to Disneyland and had just stopped for pops and chips. Danny and Luvia had just changed seats.

"If you are ever in Las Vegas you should come see us. Heidi remembers you. We talked about you the other day."

"Our paths will cross again," I said.

Chapter 16

When one tugs at a single thing in nature,
he finds it attached to the rest of the world.

John Muir

Strangely intersecting paths were, by now, a common occurrence. Another sister and I had finally made phone contact, hastened by a young man named Fabio in Italy who read the Gregory article and contacted Bonnie. When she contacted Rick Miles, he knew about the article because I sent it to him in 2005. He gave it to her, and she finally called. There are usually less than six degrees of separation in the human family.

Within less than two months of my first phone contact, I met face to face with four men who were in Vietnam with my brother. I didn't have to go out of my way because we were in the same places at the same time. Three months earlier I might have passed any of them on the street not knowing the depth of our connections. Within the first five months, I was in touch with seventeen Kilo Company veterans. All of this is thanks to the web, both the internet and the one that weaves all life together. And small acts can have big consequences along the strands of that web.

Prior to my pregnancy, my husband and I decided that the baby would have my last name. Michael's son John, from his previous marriage, already carried his last name, but I was the last to carry on the Christian name. It was Michael who suggested that it would be nice, if the baby were a boy, for him to carry the first name of my dad and brother, and so he became Robert Lucas Christian. If those decisions hadn't been made, I might not have ever connected with these men.

After I got back from that first meeting with Pete Waldinger, I wrote, "Thanks again for dinner. It was nice to meet you. It must have seemed pretty weird for you in some ways, and I appreciate your willingness to do it anyway. Watch out for those wacko Unitarian Universalists. They are especially dangerous in your area."

He wrote back:

It was a pleasure to meet you and reconnect with Tom after all these years. It did not seem the least bit weird. I am more humbled by the effort you both made to find me. What might have been weird, however, was when I got home. Jeanne asked if you had come to Boston expressly to meet Tom and me. I explained your UU ministry connection and she said, "They're one of my clients, one of my best consulting teams is working with them."

Glenn Keith later told another small-world story. Through the internet, he made contact with Al "Doc" Seguer. He didn't know Doc because they were in different platoons, but he made plans to meet him at a restaurant. Glenn arrived and saw a guy in the appropriate age range sitting at the bar.

"Doc, is that you ... Vietnam 1969?" he asked.

The man seemed surprised but nodded. Turns out he was an Army medic in Vietnam in 1969. A little later, the Navy Corpsman Glenn was waiting for showed up.

The first picture sent to me was the one that captured the t-shirt trade-off between Les and my brother. It showed Bobby and Les with two younger men, Danny Gallagher and Buck Albright. Not long after, David Crawley mentioned to me that Buck Albright was from Tempe, Arizona, but I didn't make the connection to the guy in the picture. Some months later, while visiting my ex-husband, Michael, in Tempe, I mentioned that one of the Kilo Company guys was from Tempe, but I couldn't remember his name.

When I got home, I found the name and called and left a message on Michael's message machine. He called me right back. "I went to high school with Buck. He was a year ahead of me in school," he said. Like our own son, Luke, Buck was in the Tempe High School band.

Lou Buell wrote me about going to a mall in Rochester to pick up a sandwich. There was a picture of The Wall on an easel outside of a store. "Even with 58,000 names, I wanted to check to see if any of us were on it. Just above the flag tip on the left is Gerald L. Thomas. I must have turned white because the lady came out of the shop and asked if I was OK. I told her the circumstances and that I was the one who called in the medevac for Tex and was about 20 feet from him when he was killed."

Tex was one of those colorful characters who had a way with words and a penchant for singing "God Didn't Make Little Green Apples." According to Glenn Keith, when Tex was wounded, he was "upbeat and joking that the wounds were his ticket home, based on the fact that he only had about two months left on his tour." The guys put Tex on a poncho and carried him over to be evacuated and set him down on another landmine.

Unbeknownst to the other guys, Sgt. Bill Dodson saved Tex's dog tags. At the Kilo Company reunion in 2008, we made a pilgrimage to The Wall. Bill had a container with the dog tags and a picture, which he left below Tex's name.

About a year into this journey, I sat down at a large round table in a ballroom at a hotel in Phoenix where I was attending a church conference. The woman on my right was the Rev. Mary Samuels. I told her that I had a sabbatical coming up and she asked about my plans. When I told her that I was writing a book about being in touch with men who were in Vietnam with my brother and that my son and I were going to Vietnam to visit the place where he died, her demeanor changed. We fell into a sacred space and the rest of the room disappeared. Mary was a Navy nurse in Vietnam.

When she came back, she felt the isolation that many of our veterans felt.

"No one was prepared for a woman who had been to Vietnam," she said. "When I would go to parties, I could pick the veterans out from across the room. It was in their eyes. I would walk across the room and tell them that I had been a Navy nurse. They would do this." Her shoulders relaxed. Later I told this to a few veterans who just nodded their heads. They know the look and the relief of being seen and known.

Around the time of my first visit with the guys in Boston, a man named Connie Wilson walked into an emergency room in Flint, Michigan. The doctor, who was doing a rotation at the hospital, was named Wendy. She seemed young to Connie so he started "checking out her bona fides" and found out that she had been a Navy doctor for five years. He told her that he was a Marine 3/1 Vietnam veteran. Wendy told him that her father, John Regal, also served with that company and that he was searching for other Kilo Company vets. She got Connie's permission to pass on his name to her dad.

When John Regal returned from vacation in June, he sent out an email to some of the Kilo Company guys telling them about the coincidence and telling them that Connie mentioned a 2nd Lt. Robert Christian. Tom O'Connor received the email and forwarded it to me.

Lou Buell tells a story about Robert I. "the Hawk" Widger, who had a copy of the *New York Times* that his parents sent him. He was "steamed about how they portrayed us back home." Widger said, "That's it. I am writing the Editor and all I'm going to say is 'Who gives a shit about the Marines in Vietnam? You certainly don't.'" A couple of months later, he "was jumping up and down with a paper in his hand. On the front page of the New York Times was a message in the upper right hand corner that read, "WE CARE LCPL WIDGER – THE EDITOR."

We care. Before that email message from my son, I would have guessed that there were Marines who still remembered my brother. I would have guessed that a lot of his old friends would remember him, but I never would have imagined the extent of that remembering or the pain still attached to those memories. Very few months go by that do not bring some new revelation or contact.

The younger brother of a girl Bobby dated in high school wrote:

Whenever I am in Washington D.C., I go down to the Wall and spend some quiet time there. Right after the Wall went up, Lilli-Ann went down and made some rubbings and sent one to me. I don't fully understand why Bob's life and death galvanized such feelings in me for so long. Even to this day, I find it very hard to talk or communicate regarding Bob. It is quite painful and my sadness is something I keep mainly to myself...

I came across another website with a tribute written to my brother by Jason R. Stewart, the son of one of Bobby's high school friends. He wrote, "My Father has a rubbing with your name he keeps in his desk, he talks about you sometimes. My Grandmother does too, and she cries."

A high school classmate of Bobby's found me through the www.virtualwall.org website and wrote about visiting the traveling Wall. "Knowing someone like that and then seeing their name on that monument, made all those other thousands of names become real people—fathers, brothers, lovers, and friends." She offered to send pictures from my brother's high school yearbooks.

My research also turned up a piece in the Boulder City newspaper about a new local memorial at the high school, and I wrote the author about my experience on Inis Mor, where the names of those who died at sea were remembered generations later. I wondered who might remember my brother. The letter was published, and the mother of one of Bobby's close friends, the one with the twin boys, got in touch.

It will never be written on the front page of the *New York Times*, but a lot of people still care. And with the internet, it is much easier to find those who do.

Early on, I began searching for H. Larry Kline, the Marine my sister referred to in her article and whom I assumed was the Marine who came to visit after my brother died. Then one day I remembered a box of letters that I hadn't looked at in years. Everything I needed to find those guys and others was right there. My sister had misspelled Larry's name. It was Klein, not Kline. With that correction and other information I found, I was able to track down a likely Klein, and I wrote him a note.

"I looked at that note and wondered how many other Larry Kleins had gotten a note just like it," he said when he called.

He was planning a trip to Las Vegas soon, so we met there and spent an afternoon and evening together, walking miles up and down the strip, stopping in front of the Bellagio to watch their fountain show in which the water and lights are choreographed to move to a musical score. Suddenly, Lee Greenwood's voice came booming out of the speakers, and when he got to the lines, "I'm proud to be an American, where at least I know I'm free. And I won't forget the men who died, who gave that right to me," we just looked at one another wide-eyed.

In December, 1968, Bobby and Larry Klein and Tom O'Connor flew to Vietnam on the same flight. Bobby told Larry that he was going to try to get assigned to Reconnaissance, an elite force known for its small, specialized, and high-risk assignments. Larry said, "You're crazy, but I'm in." When they got there, there were seven openings and ten or twelve guys who volunteered. Their names were put in a hat. Larry's name was drawn, but Bobby's wasn't. Larry tried, without success, to withdraw his name since the point had been to stay together and there were other volunteers. Larry has thought of what might have happened if he hadn't volunteered and if Bobby's name had been drawn instead.

"We both thought alike and acted alike. I have no doubt that if I had taken his spot and he had taken mine, he would be alive and I would not," he said. I thought of the guilt Bobby would have had if he had lived and Larry had not, knowing that he was responsible for Larry putting his name in. Men were carrying a lot of guilt for lesser reasons, that's for sure. Just surviving when others did not gives most reason enough to feel guilty.

Drew Solberg, who was there the day my brother died, wrote me several times about feeling guilty even before he wrote about "that day."

> As for those who served in combat with me I think of them all the time. I have so often over the years wondered why I came home alive and so many of the others in my unit didn't and wonder how many of them would have made more of a difference in the world than I have. I mean…here I am…disabled and not worth much of anything and how many of those young men would have been a doctor or something equally important? I do feel sad about that most of the time.

Although Larry has a 30% disability for hearing loss (he was deaf for three days in Vietnam) and for prostate cancer, which is assumed to be caused by Agent Orange, he did an entire tour with Recon without losing one man. I hadn't thought such a thing even possible.

Larry later wrote me, "I took at least two things away with me. 1. you are certainly Bobby's little sister, and 2. if I only had Bobby for a brother for a short time in my life, I'm glad to have a little sister like you now." He ended it using the nickname for me that my brother used when he didn't call me Tico. "Take care kiddo," he wrote.

When the contacts began, I didn't hold out much hope of finding the young Marine who visited us with his wife and new baby shortly before Bobby's death, and I didn't think I would ever know who the guy was who went to language school instead of my brother. I was wrong on both counts.

In that old box of letters was the folded photocopy of a letter from Skip Conover that I had never seen. It was written to my sister just weeks after my brother died and was obviously in response to her inquiry about what he had told the family about my brother giving up his place in language school. His version was only a little different than I remembered. An internet search turned up information on his book, *Tsunami of Blood: How Fear-mongering Politicians, Hate-mongering Theologians and Irresponsible Press are Guiding Us to an Age of Horrors.* Well, I guess that about says it all.

"When I saw your email, tears came to my eyes. It is still a raw wound," he said. "I was in language school when I heard Bob had been killed. I was torn apart. I remember I told your family that if I had a son, I would name him after your brother, but I never had a son. I was one of five who scored high enough on the language aptitude test to go to language school. Your brother was first in the platoon and could have had any MOS[1] he wanted. He changed his MOS to infantry which opened up the language school assignment to me. He never discussed that decision with me."

"Do you remember Bobby calling his dad and telling him he wanted out?" I asked.

"That rings some bells, but only slightly. I was going through some stuff at that time, too. I knew the war was bad in 1962. My dad took me down to the dock in Tokyo Harbor and pointed out a ship of Marines going to Vietnam. He said, 'Everyone has been or is going or will go.' When I asked, 'Why?' he said, 'Because the Generals need a war.'"

"But you enlisted?"

"After the Gulf of Tonkin Resolution in 1964, I watched the guys lining up to get married so they would be exempt from the draft and I thought 'those people are cowards.' There was never any doubt that I was going into the military."

---

1   Military Occupational Specialty.

By the time Skip got out of language school, the war was winding down, and he served a tour without injury. He works with multinational companies and has traveled to Saudi Arabia and India many times. His wife had just returned from Hanoi where she was doing a job with Microsoft.

Others, reading my entry on a few websites, have found me. In the summer of 2007, I received a letter from a woman who wrote my brother for a few months while he was in Vietnam. She got his name from a friend who was dating someone who was in his Basic School Class in Quantico. She remembers details about his life, including the name of the girl he almost married. She wrote, "I cannot explain why after 38 yrs I have a need to connect to someone in his family even though I never met him."

She doesn't have to explain it to me.

Chapter 17

Every parting is a form of death, as every reunion is a type of heaven.

Tryon Edwards

If two years earlier, someone had told me I would someday wear a nametag with skull and crossbones on it, I would have been more than a bit skeptical. Of course, if fifteen years earlier someone had told me I would go from a minister's retreat to a Marine Corps reunion, I would have suggested they look for the pod because it would be a sure sign that aliens had inhabited my body. And what if someone had predicted that I would feel totally at home in both gatherings?

The ministers' retreat in September, 2006, was at the Daughters of Mary and Joseph Retreat Center on a hill in Rancho Palos Verdes, California. Retreats begin with what is called check-in, where we sit in a circle and each speak for a few minutes about how it is with us.

"I'm angry in a way I haven't been in a long time," I said. "I'm not mad at these guys for having lives, but I'm mad my brother was robbed of his life. And seeing them all will remind me of that."

Finally, in the stillness of the chapel, there was time to think—and to just be. The constant demands of ministry combined with preparations for the retreat and reunion hadn't allowed for much of that in the past few weeks. I closed my eyes. Tears came and with them, the memory of my brother's letter from boot camp in the summer of 1967, written to our older sister:

> They let us go to church today. Most of the guys cried. I had tears just streaming off my nose into my lap during the silent prayer. I don't know what it was that got into everybody; maybe that it was the first chance we had to think in two weeks; maybe the thought of church back home, and the thought of looking at several hundred young men and knowing a lot of them are going to die for something they don't know much about. . . knowing we are being conditioned and trained to do something without thinking . . .

But my brother did think. Why was he put in a position which required him to stand against his father, his culture, his country, and probably his church, in order to be true to some inner voice that poured itself out in letters and in poetry? My anger over that had helped shape my life and my life's work.

But this time there was another dimension to the anger that I could finally express. I was angry that he didn't stand against his father and anyone and everyone else to stay true to that voice within. I wanted to rewrite history and have him do just that. What would it have taken for him to be able to do that? What would the cost have been? Going back can change the way we go forward, but it can't change history.

I walked out of the sanctuary into the breezeway, my heart and eyes full. If my colleague Rod Richards was surprised by my sudden presence beside him, he didn't show it.

"Rod, do you suppose it is harder for a daughter or son to disappoint a father?" I blurted the question out, thinking of the ways that I, but not my brother, had challenged our father.

"It may be harder for a son, but it is practically inevitable," he answered without missing a beat.

We spoke for a long time about the relationship of fathers and sons and mostly about what it means to be a man.

Six months later, I spoke to my ministerial colleagues about this journey and my conversation with Rod. I invited them to remember phrases that spoke to them and then to speak those phrases into the silence after my presentation. One of my older male colleagues sobbed as he spoke the question, "What does it mean to be a man?" It may be the most important question of our time.

After lunch on Wednesday, I left the minister's retreat and drove down the coast past Camp Pendleton to the hotel in Oceanside. Registration was in the hallway in front of the hospitality room. My nametag, made to hang around my neck, featured the 3rd Battalion/1st Marine Regiment/Kilo Company Vietnam logo with skull and crossbones and the words "TIP OF THE SPEAR." The tip of the spear, like the Marine Corps, is the first to go in. Underneath was written:

KILO COMPANY 3/1 REUNION

JAN CHRISTIAN

SISTER OF

LT CHRISTIAN KIA 4/69

When I walked into the hospitality room, Les Levy rose and enfolded me in his arms. His friend Jack Watson, an Army pilot rescued by the Marines after being shot down, had come to take pictures. They walked me over to the large banner with the Battalion Landing Team logo and the words "DEATH BEFORE DISHONOR" for the first of many pictures.

Les unfolded one of his maps from Vietnam. I had the primitive map that Tom Hobbs drew on a piece of lined paper. Tom had nailed it. I pointed to the grid that matched Tom's map.

"That is where I am going in January," I said.

A guy at a nearby table overheard and said to the guy next to him, "She has balls."

Suddenly, I was being hugged from behind. I turned in my chair. Captain John Regal, whom I had not yet met, said, "It's been a long time since I've hugged a pastor!"

John commands respect. Unlike some officers, he doesn't need patches from every Marine operation sewn to his jacket or his cap or gold-plated dog tags. He is shorter than my 5' 9" and of slight build. When he enters a room and says in a clipped Texas accent, "Let me have yer attention fer a minute," the entire room falls silent. Every eye is on the skipper. He is in constant motion. He moves among the men like a mother hen, checking on this one and then the next. At one point, he came up next to me and kissed me on the cheek. "You doin' okay?" he asked.

He, more than anyone else, is responsible for this gathering, having located over four hundred Kilo Company Marines. "I first started a few years ago looking up the guys who were with me. Then I started trying to gather them all together. I don't know if it is for me or for them or both," he told me one night.

"Probably both," I answered.

"They sacrificed everything. They came home to an ungrateful nation. We have laughed together and cried together. I have cried. Emily has cried. She wonders why I do it."

"I don't wonder," I replied.

Later he wrote, "Calling these guys cold turkey is not easy... either for me, but particularly for the guys who have in many cases not talked to anyone from the company since Vietnam. The one I located yesterday was initially confused, then elated, then started crying. This has happened many times. Sometimes I cry as well. Emily has asked me more than once why I keep beating myself up doing this but I just can't stop. Maybe I'm obsessed with finding our guys and welcoming them home."

That night John played a DVD with pictures from the guys set to music. "Tonight We Ride" was the first song, and it captured that sense of bravado that war requires. The faces and eyes were bright. The music and the pictures grew more somber. The eyes of these young Marines were now the kind a Navy nurse would later pick out of the crowd. I couldn't place the tune, but it was haunting. The next song told about a young and pretty girl who will die before her time and a dying father, but the singer knows "there's a better life for me and you."

This song by Eric Burden and the Animals also ended the DVD. Old pictures were replaced by a video taken when some of the Kilo Company men returned to Vietnam in April, 2006. The guys were in a van with two puzzled-looking Vietnamese. What the old Marines lacked in talent, they made up for in enthusiasm as they sang, "We've gotta get out of this place, if it's the last thing we ever do."[1]

When the DVD ended for the second time, Les, who was sitting across the table from me, broke my trance by asking, "How is this journey?"

With tears in my eyes, I croaked out, "Mostly good." But I was thinking about our young men and women in harm's way. I mumbled something about wishing we wouldn't send anyone under the age of forty to war. Les began to tell me why that is not practical, but I interrupted him. "Oh, I know why we mostly send our young people," I replied, remembering that we even use the word "infantry."

That night, I dreamt that I was in the back seat of a car that became airborne and was turning end over end. The driver called to me, "Are you okay?" My calm answer was, "It's a little soon to tell."

I awoke, of course, before the car landed. Dreams like this always wake us up, leaving the ending to our imagination. There is great wisdom in this. We live in uncertainty. We can live with the illusion that we control all outcomes, or we can live knowing that much is beyond our control and focus instead on how we will live well in that uncertainty. Will we deepen our illusions and build

---

1   Barry Mann and Cynthia Weill. *We Gotta Get Out of This Place.* Perf. The Animals. MGM, 1965.

walls and put our faith in preemptive strikes or three strikes and you are out, or will we open our arms and hearts to create something new?

My youthful faith was in the ability to predict and control. My youthful faith was in the infallibility of persons and institutions of authority. It was in the ability to defy death rather than to affirm life. Now my faith is in the possibilities inherent only in uncertainty. Now my faith is in the grace that is available to me in each moment, even as the car goes end over end and falls silently to earth.

I awoke with my heart pounding. I sat up and heard the question again: *How is this journey?* I came up with a wiser answer in my sleep: It's a little soon to tell. It's all up in the air. Nothing is settled. It is all still unfolding. Even my past is being rewritten.

I slept late the next morning instead of getting on the bus to Camp Pendleton to see the newest oh-so-young crop of Marines and the latest weapons of destruction. We were not visiting with the current Kilo Company. It was this Company allegedly involved in killing civilians in Haditha in November, 2005. I didn't hear them mentioned during the reunion.

After lunch, Tom O'Connor rode with me to the chapel for the memorial service, and I sat with him and Norm Hepke and Les Levy. My brother would approve of the way his Marine brothers have taken me in.

The cross was camouflaged into cross beams as a nod to pluralism, I suppose. I imagined a sanctuary with other symbols hidden into the décor, sort of like those "Seek and Find" games in the magazines at the dentist's office when I was a kid. The religious language of the service made no such nod. We spoke and sang of God the Father and prayed in the name of Jesus Christ.

Some of the early comments were of the "George Washington never told a lie" variety, the kind of thing that is designed to engender respect, but that always makes me want to jump out of my skin and take someone with me. One guy said that, in the Marine Corps he knew, no one ever smoked dope. I thought of one of my brother's letters about a guy being in the brig for that very thing.

But Pat Murphy, now a judge, spoke of a time when Republicans and Democrats watched election returns together and when it was bad taste to wear your religion on your sleeve. "Faith did not start with the 700 Club," he said. "We came from different religions and I think that's a good thing."

He called it a "long, hard, savage war." The Marines didn't begin it or set the terms for its ending, "what they did was just exactly what they were asked to do." It would be arrogant, he said, for him even to try to "explain the inexplicable." He spoke of "one nation, under God, *seeking* liberty and justice for all."

Later I told him how much I appreciated what he said about religious differences. He thanked me.

"I also like the way you held the ambiguity. Do you know what I mean?" I asked.

"Oh, yes I do," he smiled. He wiped beads of sweat from his face. Holding the ambiguity can be hard work.

The names of one hundred and fifty-nine Kilo Company Marines and six Corpsmen who died in Vietnam were read. Bagpipes played.

Chris Giordano came forward, looking boyish. Though missing his left arm, he had demonstrated the night before that he is a one-armed hugging machine. Chris was gone from Vietnam by the time my brother got there but he greeted me enthusiastically.

Chris told of playing cards with Doc Barrett on the deck of a ship when they heard the words, "Corpsman up!" Doc was sitting cross-legged and shot up as if propelled by cannon. By the time Doc's cards fluttered to the ground, he was out of sight. Later, Doc and Chris were wounded on the same day. In spite of his own wounds, Doc could see that Chris was in real trouble and needed plasma. He was able to reach Chris's foot and was trying to start a line when he took a bullet to the head. Chris later contacted Doc's father and found that he later lost another son, also a Corpsman, in Vietnam. Since the reunion, Jack Stubbs, who lives in New York near where they are buried, goes on Memorial Day to tend those graves.

Dennis Daum spoke of being hit and trying to crawl to his friend Charlie, who was mortally wounded. In April, 2006, Dennis went back to that spot and buried a Kilo Company coin and tried to bury his guilt as well. He thanked John Regal for organizing the trip.

Others got up and struggled through tears to honor those who had fallen. Jack Stubbs walked Randy Schmidt or Smitty up to the front. I knew Randy was there and planned to introduce myself at some point. Since Randy is blind, I figured I could probably pick the time and place.

I had first heard Randy's name from David Crawley, who had written me that my brother was OK, "as far as officers went." I laughed out loud when I read that. I knew this was a guy who calls them like he sees them. Later he wrote me that it was liberal thinking like mine that lost the war in Vietnam. It wouldn't have done any good to tell him that thinking like mine would have kept us out, because David would not have seen that as a good thing. His email tag-line sometimes reads, "Except for ending slavery, Fascism, Nazism and Communism, WAR never solved anything." I wrote back:

> Just to set the record straight, I am **not** a liberal. I am a radical.
> We crazy Unitarian Universalists also have a saying that "We need not think alike to love alike."
> And even though we don't think alike, I think something more important connects us. How's that for crazy?
> Take care of your bad self.

David answered, "Amen." And that exchange captures the beauty of this journey for me.

Right after my first contact with David, he had called Randy to see if he remembered my brother. Randy said, "That was the officer who pulled me off the helicopter!"

My brother kept Randy back from the patrol when Danny Gallagher was killed and David Crawley was badly wounded, and Randy was angry about it and carried guilt thinking that if he had been there, it might have been different. I understood Randy's situation, but from what I knew, I thought my brother was right. Randy was gradually losing his sight in Vietnam as a result of an earlier injury in the field. One guy told me that once they were on night patrol and the signal came to halt. Randy just kept going into the guy in front of him, and when he hit him, he just went around him, thinking he had hit a tree. Another time he walked into a water-filled bomb crater in full gear and almost drowned.

I knew that Randy knew I was there, and I wondered what he would say. He spoke of two times when Danny saved his life, both involving water. Then he came to January 21, 1969. My brother had asked for volunteers to stay behind.

"Unbeknownst to me, Danny and Chuck went to the lieutenant and told him that Smitty should be the one to stay behind. I didn't know about that when he singled me out," he said.

Randy admitted he was "unprofessional and not appropriate," and that my brother ended up giving him a direct order. All these years, Randy said, he has "carried a lot of thoughts" about how things might have been different for Danny if he had been there.

That evening, after the memorial service, I introduced myself to Randy and he gave me a big hug and asked if he could get a picture of the two of us together, but it wasn't until a year later that he told me how nervous he was that day.

"I knew you were there when I got up to speak. I really hadn't worked all that out until the reunion," he said. "I hadn't come to terms with it until then. And I felt bad after I got home from Vietnam that I had never apologized to your brother. I'm the kind of guy who will think about something and if I've done something wrong, I'll apologize and I heard after I got home that he got killed and I never got a chance to apologize. How could he know? I just reacted emotionally. I just needed to be out there with the guys. I was at a game recently and I had my Marine t-shirt on and this kid came up to me and said 'Semper Fi' and I asked him if he was a Marine and he said, 'Yes, I'm just back from Iraq.' 'Oh, that's good,' I said, 'You are back and you are okay.' He said 'Well mostly. I'm missing a leg. And now I'm being honored and all I feel is guilty because I should be with my men.' I told him, 'Your job was to be with your men and you did it. Now your job is to be stateside and take care of yourself and get healed.'"

"Randy, I think my brother understood the need to be with his men very well. I think that is exactly why he was where he was on the day he died," I answered.

I walked out of the chapel into the sunshine. Chris Giordano appeared and walked into my arms. His body shook with silent sobs. I closed my eyes and tried to will some of the peace I was feeling into his body.

Later he apologized. "You sure don't owe me an apology," I said.

"I just needed a hug," he said. "And I needed it from you."

We offer something both real and symbolic to one another, these men and I, and we are all humbled in that embrace.

And out beyond that embrace, the world keeps calling, "Corpsman up!"

Chapter 18

But faith is not necessarily, or not soon, a resting place.
Faith puts you out on a wide river in a little boat, in the fog, in the dark.

Wendell Berry, *Jayber Crow*

Weeks before the reunion, someone forwarded an email to me from Ray Kobzey. When I wrote introducing myself, he replied that he did not know my brother, but that in early April, 1969, a few weeks after joining Kilo Company, his platoon was called to a firefight in which two Company members had been killed. Their bodies were "lying in an open rice field."

"We picked up the body of a young 2nd Lt. and carried him from the battlefield where he had fallen, to the Command Post," he wrote.

For years, Ray, one of the few Canadians to serve in Vietnam, wondered who that young officer was. Based on recent research, he concluded that it was my brother. When he heard that I would be at the reunion, he planned to come and tell me that story.

I was not sure how you would receive this information, if it would cause you more pain, or if it might be a comfort to you to know that, even though the battle was still underway, your brother Robert's Marine Brothers removed him from the battlefield, to a place of dignity, as soon as they were able to do so. We were faithful.

We were faithful.

"It is unfortunate," he continued, "that I did not know Robert, but I have never forgotten him. I have made sure that my family and my friends, here in Canada, know of him and that, in my house, he is not forgotten. I feel blessed to now be able to put a name to that young man."

Ray and his wife, Margaret, sat down with me in the hospitality room at the reunion and Ray immediately began to describe that day and that body. It was heavy. There is a good reason for the expression "dead weight." It was all that he and the other Marine could do to move it. The fallen Marine was blond and had "a chest wound you could see through." There was officer insignia on the collar.

I explained that my brother had brown hair and died of a head wound. Except for the insignia, this sounded like the body of Johnnie Lee Anderson or perhaps a Marine officer killed on April fifth. Later Tom and Les said that there was no way Bobby wore officer's insignia in the bush because doing so would have made him an obvious target. Men aren't even supposed to salute officers in the bush because it draws attention to their status.

Connie Wilson was at the reunion. This is the guy who walked into an ER in Flint, Michigan, and spoke my brother's name. During my first phone conversation with him, he recited a litany of afflictions. He has cancer that might be a result of exposure to Agent Orange. He is diabetic and has problems with his left leg. He sustained head wounds in Vietnam and still has trouble remembering things. When he came home, he painted his basement black and spent eight years in therapy.

Another veteran had told me that there were no black men out on patrol the day Bobby was killed. This was in response to my question about the race of Johnnie Lee Anderson. The veteran told me, "It's a long story, but I know there were no blacks out there that day." So as I began my discussion with Connie Wilson, a black man, I assumed that he was not present that day, but that is not the way he remembered it.

"Your brother asked one of the brothers to walk point, but the guy wouldn't go so Bobby went instead. I told that man, 'You have to follow orders,' but he was scared."

"What was his name?" I asked.

"Uh, I'm not sure, but he died later."

"How do you know this?" I asked.

He began sobbing. "Because I was right there." More sobs. "Your brother died in my arms." He tried to squeak out some more words. It took him a few tries before I understood that he was saying, "I will call you back."

I hung up the phone and just stared at it for a few minutes, wondering if he meant minutes, hours, or days and knowing I would just sit there whichever it was. The phone rang almost immediately. "War isn't right. It's time for someone to say we've gotta stop killing our kids. It's only for the money. When are we gonna learn? It has to come from the top. People only do what they are told to do."

Like Tom O'Connor, Connie also remembered a black Gunnery Sergeant, a big man. "He was GySgt. Sims and he was from Detroit. I remember once he told the Captain, 'We aren't moving any further until we get a chopper in here with some food and water.'"

"Thanks for being willing to talk to me, Connie. I know it is hard."

"It might hurt but I still do it." He sounded about four years old. "I remember your brother. He was the kind of guy who never asked anyone to do something he wouldn't do." There was silence as he pictured my brother, then he added, "He had a mouth full of teeth."

"Yes, he sure did," I said laughing.

The third time I talked to Connie, he sounded like a new man. John Regal had visited him and they cried together. His cancer was in remission. "I went to the Army surplus and got my truck decorated all Marine. I call it 'The White Marine.' I wish I could drive it but I have problems with my rotator cuff on my left and also problems with my right hand. I got me a jacket that says 'Once a Marine, Always a Marine.'"

"Are you and your wife going to be at the reunion?" I asked.

"Well, you being a minister and all, I should tell you that she isn't my wife, she is my girlfriend. And yes, she and I will be there. I'll be the big happy black man."

"It will be good to see you both," I said.

"It's good to have family that isn't really family," he replied.

"Yes, Connie, it sure is."

And so here was about the biggest, happiest man of any color that I had ever seen. His girlfriend, Sheila, and her son were there with him, and Sheila testified to the change she has seen in Connie since he made contact with his Marine brothers.

What happened that day? Did Ray Kobzey carry my brother's body out of the rice paddy? Did my brother really die in Connie Wilson's arms? To ask what really happened is to miss the point and the greater truths. My brother died in Connie's loving embrace. Ray carried a Marine brother out of a rice paddy in early April, 1969, and never set him down. Others carry their own truths, and some of those truths are a lot harder to carry than others.

In August, 2008, at the next Kilo Company reunion, Wayne Sandlin and Drew Solberg took me aside to tell me that second platoon was sort of a renegade platoon, unused to taking orders and that my brother, being new, was not trusted. They saw an enemy soldier and started to follow him. When Bobby ordered them not to pursue him, they ignored the order and walked into an ambush. Others are still not able to talk about my brother or that day. Another man had already rotated back home but holds himself responsible because he wasn't there. In his first phone call to me, he kept claiming that the connection was lost, but it seemed to be his inability to continue that was interrupting the conversation. His ex-wife, a childhood sweetheart, still holds out hope for his healing and tells me, "Don't give up on him." At another reunion, a man sat across a large round banquet table from me, too far away to carry on a conversation. Just as I was leaving, he approached me, introduced himself, apologized for not being in touch sooner and then began sobbing as his son, in his Marine uniform, stood silently by his side.

On Friday I walked through downtown Oceanside, which was no longer the run-down, edgy seaside town of my memory, and called my ex-husband from the end of the pier.

"I spent my eighteenth birthday on that pier and shipped out to Vietnam the next day," he said.

I paced the pier. No doubt my brother walked that pier and thought about his dream to sail around the world. He and thousands of other boys had walked that pier wondering what awaited them beyond that horizon.

Later, I joined Ed Doyne and Arturo Alvarez who were hunched over Ed's computer in the hospitality room. I had talked to Arturo before the reunion. He was in Tom O'Connor's platoon and lives in San Antonio, Texas. Ed Doyne was in TBS with my brother and Oliver North. Ed said North had been awarded "The Spring Butt Award" for his practice of springing out of his seat and introducing himself and asking questions of any visiting dignitary. Ed lives in Seattle and was sharing pictures of his home with sweeping views of the harbor and the city skyline. I told them about my call to my ex-husband.

"How many times have you been married?" Art asked.

"Just the once," I said.

Art held up four fingers to indicate his marriages and said, "Before my last divorce, I went in for counseling. I argued with the guy about whether or not I have PTSD. He said, 'Why do you think you are on medication?' I said, 'For depression? For insomnia? For anxiety?'"

We laughed.

Two of his cousins served in Vietnam and one is 100% disabled due to PTSD. "The other checked himself into the VA psych ward in 2000. This really shocked me. He didn't seem like that kind," he said.

"I guess we are all that kind. And the people who have the hardest time are those of us who don't think we are that kind," I said.

As we spoke of the impact of war, Ed admitted that he has thought about how easy it would be to defend his home since it is on high ground. I wondered out loud if he might have been drawn to it for that reason. I spoke of veterans I know who can be standing in the midst of great beauty and think, "This would be a good place for an ambush."

"I have always taken pride in the fact that I could work with people for years and they wouldn't know I was a Marine, not that I'm not proud to be a Marine," he said. "When people find out they say, 'You couldn't have been a Marine. You are too nice.' Who did they think we Marines were, and was I not a real Marine because I am a nice guy?"

Arturo brought up the Gregory article. "It made me mad to read it. He wasn't even there when Tom rushed the bunker three times. Tom should have gotten the bronze star. I get mad every time I think about it."

Tom appeared with a plastic bag. "I got you something from Filene's basement," he said. It was two grey t-shirts, one with a collar and one without, both with the Kilo Company logo. He walked me to my car so I could put the bag in the trunk. "Now you are one of the guys," he said.

The banquet that night was at Camp Pendleton. Ray Gallegos and his wife, Sheila, and their two boys invited me to ride with them in their van. Ray, who was facing radiation treatment for prostate cancer after the reunion, was known as a man of few words in Vietnam, and he hasn't become much more loquacious over the years. After a few more reunions Ray confided in me that he will go to his grave angry that "we turned tail and ran when we could have won the war."

The boys and Sheila just took me in. Darius, who was born when many of these guys were in Vietnam, is a Major in the Army. He is dark like his father and beautiful and bright and articulate, and the guys circled around him to hear him speak in a soft voice of his time in Iraq. His mom calls him "a hillbilly Mexican." These are some well-traveled hillbillies, having lived all over the world.

Her older son, John, is the child of her first husband, another Marine, who was killed in a car accident when John was three. John, who is tall and attentive, did ten years in the Marines and then ten in the Army before becoming an EMT in Colorado Springs.

Sheila is one tough lady, having buried a husband and an adult child, who was murdered. Always impeccably groomed, she pulls an oxygen tank and speaks with authority. At the Battalion reunion a year later, she will tell men her age to take off their hats when they enter the mess hall. The young son of one of the Marines will start following her around when she tells him not to talk to his mom disrespectfully. She lets him know he is not to call her Sheila.

We sat at a large round banquet table. As the alcohol flowed, Darius became less circumspect in his analysis of the war in Iraq. He started talking about the small percentage of people who are sacrificing for their country. Sheila leaned across me and said to John, "Go make sure your brother gets some food in him." Since I was just getting ready to yell 'Preach it, Darius,' I followed them over to the buffet line. The concept of vegetarianism hasn't made it to Marine reunions, but I dug in.

Driving back, John took I-5 north instead of south, and we went seven miles out of our way in order to turn around. We all teased him, of course, but I was in no hurry. That van could have ridden off into the night, and I would have been perfectly happy. Connie Wilson is right, "It's good to have family that isn't really family."

Saturday morning I stopped in the hospitality room for some breakfast before driving down the coast to spend a night with friends in La Jolla to de-brief and decompress. While I toasted a bagel, a man began a conversation with me by saying, "I overheard that you are a minister. I'm fascinated by that because I am interested in the work of changing the minds of people."

I smiled as I read his nametag. Doc Infantati's name comes from the word "infant," which means "without speech." This is the last way I would describe Doc, who began a soliloquy about his philosophy of life as soon as we sat down, his words rushing together.

"We are living in a large liquid mind," he observed. He spoke of particles and atoms and being "our bestest, mostest, greatest" and how we are all trying to get back to that original love. "Love doesn't suck. It is how we use the present moment to subvert love that sucks." He recalled an experience after his return from Vietnam when he was playing musical chairs with the Father, Son, and Holy Spirit.

Joseph Campbell said that the difference between the mystic and the mental crack-up is that one is swimming in the water and the other is drowning, but it's the same water. Was Doc swimming or drowning? My bagel was poised in mid-air, my face frozen, my head tilted, while I considered the question.

"How do you relate all of what you are saying to your experience in Vietnam and to being here?" I asked, attempting to reel him in.

He surfaced and looked around. "The last time I saw these guys they were broken and bleeding." Tears came to his eyes. "I look around now," he said, "and I see they are strong (he flexed his arms to depict the word) and whole."

"Why did you go to Vietnam?" I asked.

"I dropped out of high school to avoid teasing and bullying and joined the Navy to see the world. I had visions of visiting Barcelona and meeting cheap women. Because of the vision in my left eye, I only had a few alternatives and being a Corpsman was one. After six months of training, I was sent to Vietnam where I was part of the machine that kept grinding out suffering and that killed three million Vietnamese, mostly civilians who were in their own country. When my daughter was a child, I took her on a roller coaster and she turned to me and pleaded, 'If there is any way you can get me off of this, please do.' That's how I felt in Vietnam."

I was miles down the freeway before I realized that there had been a lot of talk about death and dying during the reunion, but Doc was the first one who talked about killing. Keep swimming, Doc.

Tom O'Connor and Jan Christian

Chapter 19

The only journey is the one within.

Ranier Maria Rilke

In November, 2006, I was back in Boston just before my sabbatical began. I took Tom O'Connor out for dinner on the 10th, the birthday of the Marine Corps. He was a cheap date, picking a small Italian restaurant in Cambridge where we ordered at the counter. After dinner, he walked me back to the T stop and then surprised me by getting on the train with me. We got off in Boston Common and he walked me to the door of Eliot and Pickett House, the bed and breakfast operated by the Unitarian Universalist Association. It is just behind the Unitarian Universalist Association Headquarters on Beacon Street. A block up the hill is Beacon Press, also operated by the UUA. It was Beacon Press that published *The Pentagon Papers*, which earned the UUA a spot on Nixon's enemies list, a proud moment in our history.

The next day, Veteran's Day, I left South Station on the Acela Express train headed to Washington, D.C. I sat in the Quiet Car, listening to brief muffled conversations and staring out the window. A friend, Joan Bohmann, met the train at Union Station, and we stashed my suitcase in the trunk and walked to The Wall.

There were three people waiting whom I had never met. One was Greg Grisa, a local Unitarian Universalist man who had contacted me and looked up my brother's name on The Wall after reading a sermon of mine published in the newsletter of the Unitarian Universalist Men's Network. The other two were Bill and Diane Ager, my first contacts on this journey, who drove up from their home in Virginia.

The first time I visited The Wall was in the late 1980s when I was in town for a juvenile justice conference and staying at a hotel near the Pentagon. I walked the three miles with growing trepidation. The exact panel and line location were listed in the U.S. Park Service directory, but I was not prepared to see our hometown and Bobby's date of birth also listed. My stomach began to quiver, and I looked down, thinking I might be able to see it moving.

As I walked to Panel 27W - Line 55, I passed a young woman who seemed too young to even remember the war. She was crying and leaning up against the wall, her palms flat against the granite. Someone stood next to her so I kept moving. It had been years since I had shed tears for my brother, but I did that day. Someone appeared with tissues. I walked back to the hotel and sat in the lobby. A woman who was attending the conference came and struck up a conversation with me, and I told her about my visit and about the young woman.

"It was probably her father that she never knew. My dad died in World War II and I never knew him," she said.

Of course. Since that conversation, an organization called Sons and Daughters in Touch has been created to provide support to the estimated twenty thousand U.S. children who lost fathers in Vietnam.

Names of those who die from wounds sustained in Vietnam are still being added to The Wall. By the end of 2007, there were 58,256 names. Men who have died from Agent Orange-related cancer or from post traumatic stress suicides are not included.

After a warm but short visit, Bill and Diane offered the three of us a ride back to Union Station. The conversation turned to guilt. Bill said, "The older you get, the more you can see what you might have done differently." We sat in the silence. Then he added, "You could also do all the right things and still have bad outcomes."

My brother wrote something similar in a letter. It troubled him that you could get everything right and, unlike an algebraic equation, things wouldn't add up. "And it didn't help," Bill added, "that lieutenants had such a steep learning curve, and by the time they had any experience, they were usually rotated to the rear."

The next day, the first day of my sabbatical, the front page of *The Washington Post* told of Agent Orange and "war's toxic legacy." Soil near Da Nang still shows "dioxin levels...as much as 100 times above acceptable international standards."[1] An estimated twelve million gallons of Agent Orange were used as a defoliant to remove hiding places for the enemy. People still cannot hide from Agent Orange.

Later that month, I drove to Boulder City, Nevada, to stay with our former next-door neighbors, Sara and Ralph Denton. Their daughter, Sally, who is a writer, was also visiting. I went to speak about things we had never spoken about.

It is not a coincidence that veterans are beginning to gather in greater numbers now, and it is not just the advent of the web. It is that time has passed, and the passage of time provides a distance and a perspective which allows and invites introspection. Drew Solberg wrote me:

> Last week I had a very strange dream. It was a very detailed replay of the day your brother was killed. The really odd thing is that in the past those types of dreams always woke me in terror but this time it didn't even wake me. Rather when I did wake up I just lay there and let the present catch up with my brain, remembering just how vivid the dream was. I think that was because as I get older the memories of Vietnam become more persistent but I have pretty much come to accept the event as just another part of living and dying.

---

1 *Washington Post*, November 13, 2006, A1 and A17.

To dismember is to tear apart a body. Although remembering or re-membering is essential to healing, it does not guarantee it. But our remembering together in my home town was healing for me. We spoke about old hurts in ways that we could not have decades ago, and there were hurts then that I knew nothing about.

That first night, we headed down to a wine bar and café for dinner and began a conversation that continued over the next few days and later included Sara and Ralph's sons: Mark, a judge, and Scott, a pediatrician who teaches medical students.

Growing up, I was very close to all three children, usually at different times. Ralph, a local attorney, ran unsuccessfully for U.S. Congress twice. I met the Governor of Nevada, Grant Sawyer, and both U.S. Senators, Alan Bible and Howard Cannon ("If the Bible doesn't work, bring out the Cannon") in their home. The Dentons did more socializing in a weekend than my parents did in months, and I was often included in their activities as though a fourth child.

Sara and Ralph lost a son not long before we moved next door to them. One evening, around dusk, Jeffrey, a toddler, turned on the hot water in one of the bathtubs and fell in. Sara wrapped him up, and she and Ralph ran out the front door determined to carry him up to the hospital on a hill which was blocks away. The door stood open, and Mark, Sally, and Scott wandered out into the gathering darkness until a neighbor took them in.

Sally remembered the front door at dusk, both when Jeffrey fell in the bathtub and when the Marines showed up in April, 1969. Marine protocol was to go to a neighbor's house first. That night, Ralph went to their door, looked out through the glass panes, and said, "Jesus Christ, Bobby's been killed." Sara told them that Bob Christian had heart problems and that she would call our doctor and our minister.

Mark was working at Bob's Chicken Shack on the main road through town and was out emptying a mop bucket when he saw a car with Marines go by. When he got home, he saw the car and knew. "I remember Mr. Christian was in the backyard just pacing back and forth."

Scott was across town at a friend's house watching an episode of "Get Smart" when his dad showed up to get him. He still remembers which episode it was.

"That whole country wasn't worth one boy's life," Ralph said. "I tried to talk him out of going or at least not joining the Marines. Your father thought I was a traitor." Sara nodded in agreement. "We always felt that your parents moved out of the house right away because of this," she said.

I was stunned. I could picture my dad thinking that Ralph was wrong and well, yes, maybe even unpatriotic in the emotions of the times, but my mother never mentioned any negative feelings about the Dentons on her part or my father's part and often reminisced about her close friendship with Sara. Either they or I had misread the situation. If I was right about my parents, I had still failed all these years to pick up on the Denton's perceptions. Either way, I had missed something really important. What else was I missing?

Bill Ager and Jan Christian

PART III

Recovery

Chapter 20

The beginning of love is to let those we love be perfectly themselves, and not to twist them to fit our own image.

Thomas Merton

The day after Thanksgiving, I visited the Thomases. Al Thomas, who came looking for me after I ran into the night after learning of my brother's death, had died before my father. But his wife, Ruth, his son, Alan, and his daughter, Nancy, were there. It was to be my last visit with Ruth. I told Ruth about the Denton's perception. She shook her head, "Your mother just couldn't be in that house." But there was another revelation as troubling.

"Bobby planned to re-up," Nancy said. I figured she meant he intended to extend his tour in Vietnam. This was not news to me, as my sister had also told me this, but when I heard it the first time, I didn't want to consider it, because it didn't make sense to me. Nancy had her letters from Bobby and handed them to me.

I have over fifty letters Bobby wrote from Vietnam. Besides his letters home, there are the letters to Nancy, to his friend Stewart Bell and his family, to various family friends, and to Jo Schnitz, a childhood friend from El Paso, whom he had not seen in years. She was paralyzed from the neck down by childhood polio and began writing him after he went to Vietnam. Several guys mentioned that my brother was always writing letters, and my guess is that he sent dozens more. Most of the letters are less than two hundred words and fairly mundane.

My sister once chastised him for not writing about what was really going on. He blasted back a letter which said something like, "Do you really want to hear that I go out on patrol and watch my men get blown up? Do you really want to know what it's like to hold someone in your arms while they are dying or to write letters to their families?"

For the most part, he was not working through any deep feelings or reactions to what was going on. His poem was a notable exception. Mostly he was passing the time and staying connected to the world. Letters were a touchstone to connect him to another place and time. Within a few weeks of his arrival in-country, he was living for R&R. The possible spots were Hong Kong, Tokyo, Sydney, Taiwan, Okinawa, and Hawaii, but married men had first shot at Hawaii, which was his first choice also.

On January third, he answered some questions I had posed in a letter to him. "Jan, no I don't have anyone in my platoon that I already knew. No, I didn't see Bob Hope this year, but I'll have another chance next year. No, I don't know how booby traps got their name." In another letter, he told me, "No, I don't have any plans to adopt children." I guess that's what I could picture him doing. He had asked for yo-yos and strings and other stuff for kids. That I could picture. I could picture that he was playing cards and winning money.

He wrote that he was the ping-pong champion. I could picture that and I knew how one of his stories was going to end before I read it all. Just over a week in-country, he wrote, "I'm firmly established as the best ping-pong player here. I was playing last night and was only winning by one point, and every body (sic) was cheering this guy on that I was playing hoping someone could finally beat me, but the kid knew what was happening. He said, 'If I get ahead, he'll switch to his right hand, and then I'll really be in trouble.' Everyone looked over, groaned, and walked off. My radioman is the only one I can't beat left handed."

And that was another theme of his letters and his life. He wanted a challenge. He had to be in the midst of things. He did not come to a war to sit in the rear and do paperwork. He wanted to be where the action was. Another theme was his plan to get out and get "a masters degree or two" and save money to buy a sailboat. He had a boat picked out and a time-line. By 1976, he would be ready to sail the *Spirit of '76* around the world.

There it was, in a letter to Nancy on January 3: "unless I extend." Clearly, she wrote back that he couldn't do that because he responded that indeed he could. He told her not to tell my mother because she worried too much. Indeed, my mother wore her worry in the way she carried her body, but all of her worry could not save him. Worry never does.

On January 8, he admitted that he was "kind of enjoying" being in the bush. Well, it was early in his tour. But there were other references in letters that chilled me. In one, he wrote about a Kit Carson scout.

> They are VC who have come over to our side, and are working for us as scouts. Anyway I've had this one working for me that is really funny. If you can imagine this little slant eyed dude about 5' tall, telling everyone he is Mexican, and has only been in country two months. He curses in English, with an accent that is a riot. You should see him question people. He really roughs them up and works them over. When he isn't telling you he's a Mexican, he's an Indian. He really gave us a lot of laughs today.

Jo wrote him that she liked conversation and people-watching. He wrote back:

> Conversation? Try talking to the VietNamese. That is a real gas. What little English they know, what little VietNamese I know, what little French we both know, and what sign language we can dream up. It is amazing what you can get said. For instance, we were set up in this one little ville for a couple days, and one of the kids stole a can of chow that I left sitting out. I managed to tell the

old lady there that one of the kids stole my chow and that if she didn't get it back I was going to burn the whole village down. Of course, I didn't do it, but I sure had them worried!

In another letter he wrote about the danger of giving away unopened food because it might be given to the Viet Cong.

There were things I could picture my brother doing and things that I could not or would not picture. My first words when Al Thomas came to find me were, "He was so good." I didn't want to see my brother as capable of even *threatening* to burn down an old woman's village or of thinking that a scout who worked someone over was humorous. I wanted to leave this part of my brother behind, but the truth was much more complex. Of course, he was capable of these things and so much more. My gentle brother, who saved a rabbit and calmed wild hearts, including mine, was capable of that and more.

And in that silence came another disturbing truth. Anything my brother was capable of, I was, too. That and more.

More silence.

He was twenty-three. Where was I at his age? I was a correctional service officer. Kids who broke major rules lost all of their privileges and had to wear orange t-shirts. One evening, a co-worker and I brought out a whole stack of orange t-shirts just to mess with the kids and to see what they would admit to.

More silence.

And, just like him, I questioned my role in the war and the war itself, but I kept going back in.

Nothing human is foreign to me if I am not foreign to myself.

Chapter 21

Home is a name, a word, it is a strong one; stronger than magician ever spoke, or spirit ever answered to, in the strongest conjuration.

Charles Dickens

On my final day of that Thanksgiving visit in 2006, Ralph and Sara took me to breakfast and then drove me through the new veterans' cemetery and a few new neighborhoods, including one which is mostly Mormon. I understand the desire to live with those "like us," but how much richer my childhood neighborhood in Las Vegas was for its religious diversity. We attended a Presbyterian church. The Judds were Mormon and had four adopted children, and I was never in a gentler household. The Goodwins, who eventually adopted our third foster child, were Missouri Synod Lutheran, and I often went to church with them. Neighbors up the street and next door were Catholic. That neighborhood looms large in my life although I have not been back in years.

But no home has loomed larger than the white house on the hill in Boulder City. Once we moved out, I never went back in. Sara talked about various neighbors over the years and even mentioned the possibility of me going in to take a look, but I let those opportunities pass. That Thanksgiving, I realized I had less trepidation about seeking out a certain rice paddy in Vietnam than I had about walking into my childhood home.

In the film *Forrest Gump*, Jenny comes across her childhood home and, overcome by rage, she begins to pick up rocks to throw at it. She finally just sits in the dust and cries. Forrest says, "Sometimes, I guess there just aren't enough rocks." It is not bad memories that hold me hostage. For the most part, it is good memories. It is the memories of all those inhabitants and frequent visitors now dead: my father, Robert Malcolm Christian; my mother, Maxine Deas Christian; my brother, Robert Malcolm Christian, Jr.; my sister, Florence (Kris) Rosenberg; all of my aunts and uncles; many cousins and family friends.

When I got back to Ventura, I pictured going into my childhood home. Even contemplating crossing the threshold quickened my breath. I imagined standing in the doorway. When it was windy, the metal strip in the door reverberated and made harmonica-like sounds that drifted into the nearby rooms. This is the door my mother opened that evening in April. Several years before, my brother had come through that door and collapsed on the floor, crying and moaning. He and his fiancé had gone to meet with our minister to discuss their wedding, and she had announced that she was calling it off. I had never seen him cry before. I wanted to kill her.

My old parakeet, Lollipop, flew out of that doorway one Christmas Eve. That night, as we returned from visiting my sister and her family, I wondered out loud what would become of Lollipop.

"Oh, she's probably married to an eagle by now," my dad offered.

"She's probably been eaten by an eagle by now," Bobby responded.

I was both horrified and amused. When I went to my brother for comfort, it was never for the cheap variety. If I wanted to have my illusions or prejudices or self-pity reinforced, he was not the guy for the job. He always listened. Maybe he put a hand on me or put his arm around my shoulder. Maybe he just leaned in close. Maybe I played with his sleeve or worried a loose thread on his shirt while I poured out my troubles. His dark eyes that could flash so quickly in amusement would be alert and warm. "Tico," he would begin and I would feel loved and known. Wild animals grew calm in my brother's presence. We have a picture of him as a child with a butterfly resting on his shirt. He had that nonanxious presence that we ministers are supposed to cultivate. He was the eddy in the midst of the whirlpool. He was fully present to the moment. He was paying attention.

He was on my side—my best side—and I knew it. He knew what I was capable of, for better or for worse. But he saw my light even when I was at my darkest. He had faith in my ability to face facts and to choose the higher road. Sure it was painful. Yep, Lollipop was most likely deader than a doornail. Had I dissolved into tears, he would have put his arm around me, but he was not going to insult my intelligence with cheap comfort or false approval. In this way and so many others, his life prepared me for his death. He prepared me to speak truth to power. He prepared me for ministry. He prepared me to say to a teenage girl by the side of the road: *You can do this. I have faith in you.* He prepared me to go back decades later and love him for who he really was and not just who I needed him to be. To love him the way he loved me.

I did not go in the house that Thanksgiving, but nine months later I was unexpectedly back in order to meet Larry Klein in Las Vegas and to ask Ralph Denton if my dad or mom ever said anything to him directly about being angry or thinking that Ralph was a traitor. They had not.

The next morning, Sara said, "I think the neighbors are home. Do you want to see the house?"

I couldn't *not* go in. So, on my parent's wedding anniversary, I stood at the door. Even it was changed, and the other doors that used to open to the porch are now gone.

The home was a foreclosure when Mike and Sue bought it. The previous residents, who had small children, used the fireplace for cooking and heating and even burned wood from the floors because the power was turned off. Beer bottles and trash filled the toilets. Trees and grass, everything green, died.

Mike and Sue built a new home inside those walls. They opened it up. My old room is now the master bedroom. The adjacent room and bath and the former master bathroom are all now part of the master suite. My first thought was, *Wait until Mom hears this!* What was outside has been taken in. A side patio is now a family room. The home now takes greater advantage of the view of Lake Mead in the distance. There are a few reminders of the past. One of the built-in ironing boards remains.

I stood in their kitchen, close to tears. When I got back, I wrote them:

> This is a belated, but heartfelt, thank you for opening up your home to me a few weeks ago. The changes to that house in many ways mirror the changes I have experienced. It has experienced death and transformation and "my room" has expanded to contain that which used to belong to others. Some of the old ways in and out are no longer there, but new space has been taken in and the views are enriched and expanded. And, as you put it, "great care was taken to maintain the overall integrity" of the place. And so you have given me quite a gift and I am deeply grateful.

Bobby and butterfly

Chapter 22

The winds of grace are always blowing.
You just have to raise the sail.

Ramakrishna

January 1, 2007. Upon waking, with my eyes still closed, words and sentence fragments came to me. Words that didn't go together. Grace. War. I finally opened my eyes hoping to dispel the words in the sunlight. But, as my feet hit the floor, one more word came to me. Haditha. I thought of a friend's advice some months earlier: Pursue this only as long as it is life-affirming.

That strange reverie, perhaps remaining from the night's unremembered dreams, hung over me as the day unfolded. I made one of my infrequent visits to the mall for some trip-related purchases and then headed to the beach to take advantage of a minus tide and to start the year off right.

The winds of grace are always blowing.

I parked along the street at Marina Park and headed to the sand. I walked up the beach for about twenty minutes and then turned around to head back. I was on a stretch of beach between two rock jetties that had been the recent site of a memorial service for a man who went into the ocean when a small child was swept off one of the jetties by a freak wave. He saved the child but lost his own life. Two driftwood crosses, each with a pile of dying flowers, marked the area.

An older couple approached in the distance, both bundled up against the chill. Suddenly, between us, a young woman in a bikini came across the dunes, striding purposefully toward the surf. She was lean and strong and, with her long strides, quickly arrived at water's edge. She did not stop to test the water, but simply walked into the water and with a slight skip, plunged headfirst into the first wave that was high enough to take her in.

My fog lifted. I smiled and wished for a camera to capture the juxtaposition of those of us all bundled up and this young woman plunging into the waves. Something life-affirming was being modeled for me. *Keep going. Dive in.* I walked past her entry point and continued down the beach until I reached the jetty a few minutes later. There I stopped and turned back to watch her again, but she wasn't there.

I climbed onto the jetty for a better view, but I couldn't find her in the water or on the beach. My back had only been turned for a few minutes. There is no way she could have gotten out of the water and off the beach that quickly. A small boy played at the end of the jetty and I approached his grandmother and asked if she had seen the woman. No, she had been watching her grandson, Matthew. I called Matthew over, but he hadn't seen her either. The older couple was no longer visible.

Marines have reported seeing normal village life only to turn around and find something more sinister in its place. Buck Albright saw a lone farmer on a beautiful sunny morning and knew something was amiss, but he knew it too late. Was the purposefulness in her stride aimed at ending instead of affirming life? I walked up the beach again, thinking of two young people I knew who committed suicide in January, one just the year before, and an older man who committed suicide on January 1, 1969, only hours after playing golf with my father.

My cell phone was in my car so I walked back down the beach to a nearby business on Seaward Avenue to use their phone. Within five minutes, a rescue team arrived and took my information. I returned home and watched that stretch of beach, miles from my condo. Occasionally, I picked up my binoculars and watched the rescuers diving over and over again until the darkness overtook them.

"What is your book about?" Peter Haslund, the husband of a colleague and a Vietnam veteran, asked months before I began writing. After my semi-articulate rambling about it, he commented that it is my continual search that he found most interesting. That night I felt like I was searching in deep, dark water.

A few church members wrote me as my sabbatical began. Nick Williams, 93-years old and still painting houses, sent me a card about the wisdom of following my heart and wrote inside, "Don't get bogged down in a rice paddy somewhere." I knew just which rice paddy I might get bogged down in. I had the maps. I could show you the little grid. I could name the coordinates. Was I already bogged down?

I wrote another member, Jim Merrill. "I am very moved that Luke wants to go, even if it's partially because he thinks he needs to take care of his mom." He wrote back.

Pardon my dullness, but where does the "even if it's partially" come from? Jeepers, gal. You're on the hero's quest of a lifetime, and your son has the audacity to think that he might be of some assistance because (here I interpolate) he loves you and this is his way of showing it. Who needs "even if"? I'm gonna step out on a limb and suggest the obvious: this enterprise, from the reunion to the trip to Nam, requires a heaping help of humility if it is to make sense.

Out for dinner with friends, I talked about my plans to meet with a former North Vietnamese Army soldier.

"I know you have thought about what you will say," one of them said.

"No, I really haven't," I surprised myself and them by answering. "I guess what I want to say is 'I'm sorry. I'm just sorry. For their losses and mine and everyone's losses. I'm sorry,'" I stammered. We all stared into our drinks for a few awkward moments of silence.

The winds of grace are always blowing, but how to raise my sail?

I wrote a local trusted reporter about my upcoming trip. Within an hour, Tom Kisken was on the phone. He had spoken to his editor and wanted to come see me and bring a photographer, Dana Rene Bowler.

Their interest in the story grounded me once again. This was not just about me. In fact, it wasn't much about me at all. I was going to bear witness and to pay tribute. I was going for those who could not. The paper ran a story and one of the pictures showed me at a candlelight vigil protesting the planned surge of U.S. troops in Iraq. "How does this remind you of Vietnam?" Tom asked.

John Regal sent out an email of mine to the guys, and even some I didn't know sent their well wishes. I got an email from George Baldwin whom I knew had fielded some late-night phone calls from Stephen Gregory and even visited him in jail. I had tried to reach him once but didn't hear back. He wrote that he commanded 2nd Platoon until April 10, when he got called up for another job. Bobby was put in temporarily until someone else could be found. George wrote, "He was ambushed the next day walking where I would have been walking. His death has haunted me for 40 years and he was the only reason I ever found and touched a name on the wall."

I called Bonnie Anderson. On New Year's Day, she called her younger brother and talked to him for the first time in twenty-three years. Like his father, he is an electrician. He lives in Las Vegas, Nevada.

I had Pete Waldinger's maps, still in their original Ziploc bag. Tom O'Connor and I left messages back and forth and then two laminated copies of the Marine Prayer arrived in the mail. It didn't reflect my theology or my image of God and that didn't matter. What I held in my hand was sacred. My friend Catherine Rossbach insisted on taking me to LAX and promised to be there waiting upon my return.

Pilgrims of old would not think of starting their journey without a blessing, and I had received many. I was ready. It was time. A deep peace settled upon me. The winds of grace are always blowing and others raised my sail.

Chapter 23

My heart has followed all my days
Something I cannot name.

Don Marquis

On the China Air flight over, I read *A Rumor of War* by Phil Caputo. Writing about his fellow Marines, Caputo writes, "There were more admirable men in the world, more principled men, and men with finer sensibilities, but they slept in peaceful beds." These words haunted my trip. They indicted and convicted me.

We landed in Hanoi on the morning of January 15. Our guide, Huang, was waiting with a big smile and a sign. He sat in the passenger seat in front, next to our driver. Luke sat behind him and stared wide-eyed at the landscape and the traffic.

After checking into our hotel, we visited a few places in a mix of exhaustion and adrenalin created out of twenty-four hours of travel, a sixteen-hour time difference, and our first glimpse of this foreign land. There is a sweetness and mellowness to this mix for me, and the pictures of us on this day show our Buddha-like smiles. How different from what the mix of exhaustion and adrenalin created for my brother day after day.

Huang is seven years older than Luke. They immediately bonded over fashion. As Luke said into the video camera the newspaper loaned us, "Some people say clothes make the man. That isn't true. Bad-ass jeans make the man."

While touring Hanoi's first university, Huang told us of a cobra farm where tourists see cobras killed and drink their blood. Luke was immediately interested, having seen something like this in a movie. Huang asked if I wanted to do it, which gave me a chance to use the words I had memorized to help me navigate Vietnamese menus and especially a moment like this.

"Ang chay," I said.

Huang doubled over in laughter. Luke look puzzled until Huang said, "She say 'no meat.' She doesn't eat meat." We decided that this was something for the guys to do together.

Our hotel was close to a Catholic church where bells rang every fifteen minutes and provided an urgent and prolonged call to mass at five a.m., causing the air to reverberate long after the bells were stilled. The tiny breakfast room at our hotel wasn't inviting so we found a small café overlooking the church plaza.

We returned by 8:30 to meet with Mr. Son, a former NVA soldier, located for me by my travel guy. I wished for Huang to translate because the man with Mr. Son had neither Huang's English skills nor his easy way with people. Long and apparently heartfelt answers from Mr. Son were translated into short sentences.

I asked a question, even though I feared I knew the answer. "Although the official count was twelve NVA soldiers killed that day, some people have estimated that as many as sixty NVA were killed. There were probably no survivors. How long would it have been before their families were notified?" I asked.

Mr. Son spoke for a long time. His hand gestures indicated bombs falling. It may have been months or years or maybe they just never returned. When entire groups were wiped out by bombing, as was the case on this day, chances are good that no notification was ever made and that there were no bodies left to recover. By some estimates, about three hundred thousand Vietnamese people are still missing in action.

We stared into one another's eyes. Some things don't need translating.

Mr. Son fought for about a year and then was hospitalized for two years. Like Tom O'Connor and Luke's father, he was raised Catholic. He works with the Maryknolls, a Catholic mission promoting economic justice and human rights around the world. He spoke of his sons, ages twenty-five and twenty-three. I pointed to Luke and told him Luke was twenty-three, the age my brother was when he died. As we ended our meeting, he handed me two identical beaded coin purses, which he made for me. Each had a gold star on a red background representing the Vietnamese flag.

Huang picked us up to begin our tour day by going to see Ho Chi Minh. Uncle Ho, as he is still known, is a major presence in the country and is credited with winning Vietnam's independence. His picture is on all the currency and in many government buildings. In his pursuit of independence, Ho Chi Minh repeatedly sought help from the United States. After World War I, he tried to see President Wilson when Wilson was in France to sign the Armistice. After World War II, he wrote eight letters to President Truman asking for our support and equating Vietnam's struggle for independence with our own. The letters weren't answered.

In 1945, the year my brother was born, Ho Chi Minh delivered the Vietnamese Declaration of Independence. The French, he said, handed over the country to the Japanese when they invaded in 1940 and then refused to join with the Vietnamese to overthrow the Japanese. Now the Japanese were defeated, and it was time for the French, who had occupied the area since the 1850s and who "built more prisons than schools," to go. It was time for colonialism to end. The Vietnamese helped rescue U.S. fighter pilots shot down over Southeast Asia during World War II, and Ho Chi Minh hoped that a new era was dawning with the defeat of the Japanese, who invaded Vietnam in 1940.

He referred to the U.S. Declaration of Independence and the Declaration of the French Revolution and remarked, "We are convinced that the Allied nations which at Tehran and San Francisco have acknowledged the principles of self-determination and equality of nations, will not refuse to acknowledge the independence of Vietnam."

And just in case we did refuse, he added that "members of the Provisional Government of the Democratic Republic of Vietnam solemnly declare to the world that Vietnam has the right to be a free and independent country and in fact it is so already. The entire Vietnamese people are determined to mobilise all their physical and mental strength, to sacrifice their lives and property in order to safeguard their independence and liberty."

The U.S. continued to support the French even when they reneged on an agreement with Ho Chi Minh by setting up a separate government in 1946, beginning what is known in Vietnam as the French War. By the time the French were defeated at Dien Bien Phu in 1954, we had provided as much as a billion dollars and substantial military equipment. It wasn't long before we decided to go it alone. We were determined to succeed where the French, the Chinese, and the Japanese failed. The American War began.

Ho Chi Minh died in 1969, less than five months after my brother. After his death, his dream of independence was achieved but his wishes regarding his body were not. Ho Chi Minh wanted to be cremated because it is more hygienic and saves valuable farm land. He wanted his ashes placed in three urns and those urns placed in the North, the South, and Central Vietnam. Instead, he has become, as some remark, another "peasant under glass." His body is sent to Russia annually for whatever it is they do to preserve dead leaders for public viewing.

The mausoleum looks like a bigger version of the Lincoln Memorial, which is ironic given that Lincoln is the U.S. leader credited with keeping the north and south together.

I asked Huang whether or not he sees the country as reunified. He said, "Oh yes."

I thought about a television show Luke and I watched the night before about the killing fields in Cambodia. The reporter asked an old man what people thought of Pol Pot.

"Oh we liked him."

"Why did you like him?" the reporter asked.

"Because he would kill us if we didn't," the man answered.

Inspired by the reporter's wisdom, I thought to ask Huang, "What would someone from the South say about the country being unified?"

"Oh, they would say that it isn't," he quickly answered.

And in Vietnam, as in the United States, that has a lot to do with how the victors treated the vanquished after the war. In Vietnam, massive numbers of those who sided with the Americans were killed or subjected to "re-education camps." A man I know went to one of those camps for the crime of having studied in the United States. He was taken out at night to find unexploded land mines and ordnance. He and others held hands in a long line and walked across fields and they almost always found something. Those who lived went out again the next night. Others were relegated to low-paying jobs which condemned them to crushing poverty. The graves of South Vietnamese soldiers were destroyed. In a country where ancestor worship and reverence is such a part of daily life, this will have ramifications for generations. Even a distribution of Ho Chi Minh's ashes couldn't have healed that.

We stood in line and went through a security check point. No shorts. No revealing clothing. No hands in pockets. No talking. *Absolutely no pictures.* The line moved slowly up stairs, into the refrigerated, dimly lit room and around the sarcophagus and out of the room and down another staircase.

Nearby are the simple quarters where Ho Chi Minh lived. A year earlier I had visited the place where Gandhi died and saw his simple accommodations only steps away from where he was assassinated. I was struck by the similarities of their living quarters. For the first time, I considered the absolute contrast in their strategies for achieving independence and a simple question formed in my mind and startled me: *What if Ho Chi Minh had embraced nonviolence?*

There were Buddhist monks in the south who opposed violence. The U.S.-supported government in Saigon was not all that popular and for good reasons. It is not hard to get soldiers from other countries to fight against those who have demonstrated a willingness to kill, but what if they expressed a willingness only to die for their independence? How would those scenes have played out on the world stage and the nightly news?

It set off a barrage of What Ifs: What if we had been willing to take even a small percent of the estimated one hundred and fifty billion dollars we poured into that war to build a strong postcolonial Vietnam? Would we have exerted influence by example if President Truman had answered Ho Chi Minh's letters and offered our help in building on his Declaration of Independence? Or what if our support of Diem and those who came after was in the form of building infrastructure, and we had held him to free elections and other reforms?

Our next stop was the place nicknamed the Hanoi Hilton by Americans imprisoned there. To the Vietnamese, it is known primarily as the place where the French held, tortured, and killed Vietnamese who rebelled against French colonialism. There are life-sized models of Vietnamese shackled at the ankles on platforms that slope backwards so that the blood gathered in their buttocks or in their heads, depending on their positions. A guillotine serves as a silent sentinel.

Pictures of U.S. prisoners of war seek to convince visitors that the Vietnamese treated their prisoners more humanely than the French treated the Vietnamese. This may well be true, but I'm glad not to have first-hand knowledge of either approach, and it is clear that our human tendency to identify another's inhumanity while being blind to our own knows no borders.

Pictures of American demonstrations against the war covered one wall. At the top of the display were two pictures, a woman and a man. I recognized the man as Norman Morrison, a devout Quaker and father of three, who immolated himself outside of Secretary of Defense Robert McNamara's office at the Pentagon on November 2, 1965. In 1995, I read his wife's account of that day. She had no idea what he had planned when she served him French onion soup for lunch.[1] I still can't see a bowl of onion soup without thinking of Morrison.

The inscriptions were in Vietnamese, and I didn't think to ask our guide what was written there. I took a picture of the display and made a mental note to check to see if an American woman had self-immolated in protest. I didn't remember anything like that. It seemed unlikely, but what I discovered shocked me.

On March 16, 1965, eighty-two-year-old Alice Herz immolated herself on a Detroit street corner. She stated in her suicide note that she was protesting "the use of high office by our President, L.B.J., in trying to wipe out small nations." Herz's daughter said her mother's act "wasn't mental derangement or a psychological compulsion," but "the need to do something that would call attention to the gravity of the situation."

Herz attended First Unitarian Universalist Church for ten to fifteen years, and her minister called her "an intellectual 'in the best sense of the word' who was once a Quaker 'and still thinks of herself as a Quaker.'" He added, "This is not the work of a crackpot."[2] In my preparation for ministry and all my reading of Unitarian Universalist history, I had never heard of her.

---

1   http://www.sojo.net/index.cfm?action=magazine.article&issue=soj9507&article=950752.

2   http://www.angelfire.com/nb/protest/amer.html.

In this country, we seem to believe that people get the governments they deserve. People I have met in other countries seem more inclined to separate the actions of government from the intentions of the people. Although I saw plenty of examples of the devastation caused by the American War, I never saw anything that demonized the American people.

We ate lunch in the lovely courtyard of a nonprofit restaurant that prepares young adults for the restaurant business. Huang's wife got her start there, but Huang had a different savior. He shined the shoes of a Canadian man who took an interest in him and learned of Huang's story through a translator and then paid for Huang to go to school.

That afternoon Miss Giang came to our hotel and rode with us to Friendship Village, where she works. Friendship Village was founded by American veteran George Mizo. Working with the Vietnamese general responsible for killing his platoon in 1968, Mizo and other veterans wanted to create a place to help mitigate the ongoing effects of Agent Orange. Mizo has since died, but his dream is flourishing. There is a residential workshop to teach children crafts and trades that they can take back to their home communities and a residence for veterans who need some respite and fresh air.

One small girl ran out of her classroom to greet me and began shaking my hand, pumping it up and down within a two foot range. I asked her name and told her mine and pointed to Luke, who was videotaping, and told her his name. She was still pumping up and down.

"You're a good hand shaker," I said, laughing.

At that point, she dropped my hand and put her arms around me. "You're a good hugger, too. That's my first hug in Vietnam," I said, gladly returning the embrace.

An older boy, wearing a floppy hat, came and took my hand and walked with us around the grounds. Whenever I stood still, he hugged me. At one stop, after hugging me, he approached Luke, who said, "Do I get a hug, too?" He then headed towards Huang and our driver, but they quickly extended their hands to keep him at arm's length.

In Vietnam, the reminders of the American War are constant, but one of the strangest moments for me came at Friendship Village where the children flashed us peace signs. What they meant to them, I do not know. Although many of these children and veterans are suffering from the effects of Agent Orange, the extent to which Agent Orange is responsible for the children's disabilities is the subject of controversy, since the tests needed to make that determination are complicated and expensive. For the cost of determining the cause of individual disabilities, many children could be served. But it is clear that in Vietnam, the "water still runs bloody from the taps."

In 1971, in an interview with Walter Cronkite about the Pentagon Papers, Daniel Ellsberg said, "In the seven thousand pages of this study, I don't think there is a line in them that contains an estimate of the likely impact of our policy on the overall casualties among the Vietnamese or the refugees to be caused, the effects of defoliation in an ecological sense."[3]

That afternoon, Luke went off on the back of a motorcycle to drink cobra blood. He burst through the door just as I was headed to dinner and announced, "That was the coolest thing I've ever done. I think I'm going to be sick."

I ate dinner that evening with American Tom Leckinger and his Australian wife. Tom was then working for Vets for America. Their work throughout Vietnam depends upon the local needs, so, in one place, it might be housing and, in another, it might be services for victims of land mines or Agent Orange. Tom and his wife have had postings all over the world, but Hanoi won their

---

3   Daniel Ellsberg, *Secrets: A Memoir of Vietnam and the Pentagon Papers*, p. 401.

hearts. Tom had just put some veteran buddies on the train to Hue. In comparing itineraries, I discovered we were staying at the same hotel there.

On Wednesday, January 17, my birthday, we took a day trip to the hauntingly beautiful Halong Bay. Huang went with us on the boat, and we shared an elaborate meal together. As we three were the only passengers, Huang kept smiling and saying, "We VIP."

Luke tends towards silence; Huang never stops talking. We talked about vegetation, politics, values, and family. Huang's grandfather fought against the French and died younger than he should have as a result. After Huang shared details about his father, I realized that Huang's father and Luke's father were enemies fighting in the same area at the same time.

On the way home, I asked Huang what he thought about the fact that Ho Chi Minh never married. Might he have been gay?

"Absolutely not. He was too busy working for the country," Huang replied.

Earlier he had spoken about a married man and his girlfriend and said, "It is nothing serious. We have a saying that maybe you eat rice everyday but sometimes you like to have noodles."

"Maybe Uncle Ho was just 'a noodle man?'" I asked.

"Yes! Noodle man!" he laughed.

Luke and I wished for more flexibility in our travel plans so that we might have accompanied Huang to his home village outside of Hanoi where his mother rises in the middle of the night to make tofu and where his son is being raised. When we parted, Huang pointed to his eyes and tears forming there. "I love your mom," he said to Luke as he hugged me.

Then the sons of enemies embraced.

A hug at Friendship Village

Luke Christian

Luke and Huang, the sons of enemies

Chapter 24

An enemy is a person whose story we have not heard.

Gene Knudsen Hoffman

We flew to Hue. Luke stood outside the hotel while I checked in and then reported, "Some guy was talking to me and I think he was offering me something, but I couldn't understand if it was sex or drugs or just what it was."

"Did he use the expression 'boom-boom'?" I asked.

"Yeah, maybe."

"That would be sex." I answered.

We told our guide, Hieu, about this later and he laughed and advised Luke not to take advantage of such offers. A client of his took advantage of an offer and then wanted Hieu to recover his wallet when he discovered it was stolen. I had already told Luke of some advice an elderly Vietnamese woman gave me when I attended a Vietnamese Buddhist Mission near my home and spoke of my trip. She came up very close to me and said, "You tell son not go with women. Look pretty on outside but maybe not so pretty on inside. Or maybe they see son and think ticket out."

On our second morning in Hue, we spotted Tom's veteran buddies at breakfast, and they joined us. I told them a story from *Catfish and Mandala* by Andrew X. Pham. When Pham, who was brought to the U.S. as a child, returned to visit his homeland, he asked a tour guide at the Demilitarized Zone (DMZ), the line that once separated North and South Vietnam, why only Westerners take the tours. "Why do you think Vietnamese soldiers can forget more easily than American soldiers?"

> We live here. They don't. It's like, say, you and me falling in love with the same girl. We both had bad and good times courting her, maybe she hurt us both. I win and marry her. You go home to your country far away. After twenty years, all you have of her are memories, both the good and the bad. Me, I live with her for twenty years. I see her at her best and at her worse. We make peace with each other. We build our lives, have children, and make new history together. Twenty years and you have only memories. It is not the forgetting but the new history with the girl that is the difference between you and me.[1] (284–285)

I didn't do the story justice, but the guys nodded their heads. It made sense to them.

And on our second day in Hue, we headed to the DMZ to join other Westerners. Two things stood in stark contrast to the area around Hanoi. Almost every home has an outside altar, and cemeteries cover the landscape. The outside altars, outlawed for a time, indicate someone has died an unnatural death away from home.

From the back seat of the car, Luke and I drank in the country-side. Suddenly, in the far distance, I saw the figure of a woman and called out, "Quan Yin!"

"No, Quang Tri," replied Hieu referring to the province we were in.

"No, I mean Quan Yin, the Buddhist Goddess of Compassion," I answered.

"Oh, you know her?" he asked, obviously pleased. "Here she is Quan Am."

---

1   Andrew X. Pham, *Catfish and Mandala: A Two-Wheeled Voyage Through the Landscape and Memory of Vietnam.* New York: Picador, 2000.

One of the stories told about Quan Am is that she was a young woman from a poor family. One night, while her husband was sleeping, she approached him with a knife to cut a wild hair on his face. He awoke and, thinking that she was trying to murder him, sent her away. Quan Am never tried to defend herself but traveled the countryside begging for food. Eventually, in desperation, she shaved her head and entered a Buddhist monastery as a man. When she rejected the advances of a young woman in the village, the young woman went out and became pregnant and then came to the monastery with her baby and claimed that Quan Am was the father.

The baby began to cry and Quan Am picked the baby up, which was interpreted as an admission of guilt. One story has her roaming the countryside for a while before coming back and admitting her lie and asking for forgiveness for herself and for those who harmed her and then dying on the spot. Another ending is that she was beaten to death and her secret discovered as her body was prepared for burial.

What better place to discover Quan Am, "she who hears the cries of the world," than in Quang Tri Province, the most heavily bombed area in military history? There are still billboards warning of unexploded ordnance and land mines which continue to kill and maim. One of the cries she may have heard was of the newborn Hieu, our guide, who was born in 1975 at the end of the war and whose mother remembers the final shelling that accompanied her newborn's cries.

Just north of the DMZ, we joined other Westerners at the Vinh Moc tunnels, although we were the only Americans on the tour. The tunnels are composed of three levels which provided safe haven from U.S. bombing for three hundred locals. Seventeen babies were born underground. A picture showed the DMZ looking as barren as a moonscape with the caption, "Heaven Devastated."

Back in Hue, we toured the Citadel, known to Americans as the center of the Battle of Hue City, fought during the 1968 Tet Offensive. Although the North's offensive was not successful militarily, it turned the political tide in the United States, which helped inspire the North to persevere. Luke's uncle, Dan Roach, fought in that battle, which is depicted in the film *Full Metal Jacket*. I heard or saw no mention of the battle during our tour of the Citadel. Perhaps because of the mass killing of civilians by the North Vietnamese Army, they think that the less said the better. Our guide did point out a few bullet holes when I asked him about it.

On a rainy morning, we set out by boat to visit the Thien Mu Pagoda, a working monastery and home of Thich Quang Duc, the monk who drove to Saigon on June 11, 1963, and poured petrol on himself and lit a match. The car he drove that day is on display. I explained to Luke that the monk was protesting Diem's oppressive policies, especially those related to religion. I said, "Not long after that, the U.S. allowed Diem's assassination even though we had been backing him. This was shortly before Kennedy's assassination." As we walked away, we overheard a Vietnamese guide tell a group of Chinese, "and then the CIA killed Diem." OK, that was more to the point.

In Vietnam, the job of guide is separate from the job of driver. Our guides spoke good English; our drivers did not. Through Hieu, we retained our driver to take us to our next destination of Hoi An, south of Da Nang. We wanted to go over the Hai Van Pass, instead of through the tunnel, the route most buses take.

Our driver was quiet during our days in Hue, but he took his promotion to guide seriously and was very solicitous. Our first stop was at a market near the hotel so he could supply us with bottled water and wet wipes. At Hieu's direction, he took us to see a tall statue of Quan Am, a few miles off the highway, up a muddy road. She rose with such grace and grandeur out of the mud and mist that I stood outside in awe for some moments before entering at the base of the statue and sitting cross-legged in silence before the altar.

The road between Hue and Da Nang is one of National Geographic's "Fifty Places of a Lifetime." Before reaching the top, we stopped to take in the view, and a boy magically appeared selling all sorts of wonderful items that we would be foolish to live without. This included miniature tins of tiger balm which I later used as a party game to see if anyone could actually open them. Soon his uncle appeared with a tray of items. When he found out where I was from, he said, "I work Airborne Americans" and he began a litany of names and home states. Then he pointed to his milky left eye and said, "V.C. grenade. V.C. come. No good for me."

At the top of the Pass, we were accosted by women selling their wares. One pointed to her bulging belly. "I have two sons. Want daughter. North Vietnamese say sons blessing. Not for mothers. Daughters blessing." So far the conversations in the south clearly distinguished south from north.

We drove past former Marine installations in Da Nang and past Marble Mountain and China Beach before arriving at our hotel in Hoi An. The rooms were in a charming two-story building which overlooked a lawn that was manicured over the next few days with hand clippers. Beyond the courtyard was the Memory Café with tables on a covered patio. Brother's Restaurant was just down the street.

This was January 21, the anniversary of the day in 1969 when five Marines from 1st and 3rd platoons were killed and twelve wounded in separate booby trap incidents. Those killed in action from first platoon were James Wiley, Danny Gallagher, and Jim Porter. The dead from third platoon were Alva Terrell, an Arizona boy, and Don Turner. Inspired by the pictures of Danny Gallagher drinking from a glass mug, I hoisted a cold one to him and the others who died that day.

That night I read about the Battle of Iwo Jima in *Flags of Our Fathers*. There, too, the enemies were *in* the island, not just *on* the island. It was 1945, the year my brother was born, the year Ho Chi Minh declared Vietnam's independence.

Quan Am

Chapter 25

Pile the bodies high at Austerlitz and Waterloo.
Shovel them under and let me work—
I am the grass: I cover all.
And pile them high at Gettysburg
And pile them high at Ypres and Verdun . . .
Two years, ten years, and passengers ask the conductor:
What place is this?
Where are we now?

Walt Whitman

On the morning of January 22, I sat on the patio and removed a small red ribbon from the red damask napkin on my breakfast plate and put it in my pocket as a memento. My eyes took in the beautiful courtyard as I drank strong coffee and ate rich, thick, slightly sweetened yogurt. How different this morning in January, 2007, than this day in January, 1969. And yet how similar for a Marine's family somewhere. For a family somewhere, this, too, was a day to awaken to a new, unrecognizable world.

And how different this morning was from April 11, 1969. My brother's sleep was no doubt fitful. Did he even eat breakfast? He wrote a friend that he was not eating much, but not to tell his mother. Although there was little rain, the temperatures that April ranged from an average low of 73° to an average high of 88°. In this humidity, we already knew that temperatures in the seventies can be oppressive.

The official battalion documents for April, or for any other month, are about numbers:

In April 1969, the 3rd Battalion, 1st Marines was located at the Dien Ban District in Quang Nam Province of the Republic of Vietnam. The Battalion continued its primary mission as the Mobile Battalion for the 1st Marine Regiment. During April 1st – April 30th, the Battalion conducted four battalion-sized operations; six company sized operations and platoon-sized activities, almost daily, consisting of time on target (TOT) checks and sweeps of suspected rocket and mortar sites within the "Rocket Belt." The Battalion began the month with a successful operation in the "Dodge City" area of the Da Nang tactical area of responsibility (TAOR). The Battalion spent nine days in the field on Battalion size operations. April 3rd – 12th, the Battalion conducted successful operations in the Dodge City, Republic of Korea (ROK) TAOR which resulted in the destruction of 96 enemy bunkers and 119 Viet Cong (VC)/North Vietnamese Army (NVA) killed in action. The capture of uniforms, weapons, a radio, a typewriter, foodstuffs and numerous documents. The documents identified the complex as the headquarters for the Q-82 Battalion, which had eluded the Free World Forces for many years. The Battalion sustained 18 killed in action, 101 wounded in action and two died of wounds. Non-battle casualties were five serious, eight non-serious and three deaths. One Marine officer, 54 Marine enlisted were rotated to the Continental United States (CONUS) and received three Marine officers, 97 Marine enlisted and 10 Corpsmen. Fixed wing aircraft dropped approximately 21,000 pounds of bombs and 10,000 pounds of napalm. Target coverage was good to excellent.[1]

Luke joined me for breakfast and soon our guide, Hoa, appeared. I knew that she was the guide for the Kilo Company guys who were there in April, 2006, but we were on our way before she made the connection. When she began to tell stories about

---

1   Oral History Collection: Marine Corps History and Museums Division; Vietnam CD #22. Another Kilo Company Marine also remembers that they found medical supplies sent to the enemy from Berkeley, California.

Dennis Moriarty, Luke put in his ear buds and turned up his iPod. Dennis got lots of attention on the trip because of his Buddha-like physique. One picture showed Dennis with a bare-bottomed baby draped over one of his massive arms and the baby's family, on the sidelines, bent over in laughter.

"Kilo Company drink lots of beer," was Hoa's final observation.

As we turned onto a dirt road, headed west off of Highway 1, Hoa turned more business-like, and I began to shoot pictures in sepia tones. Hoa got out with the map and looked around. Two little boys, one with a baby on his hip, came up to us briefly, but as Hoa went over and began talking to a man in his nineties, they hung back.

The man had lived in that area all of his life. Most of his beetle-blackened teeth were no more than stubs. As his wife came over to see what was going on, he pointed in two directions. Hoa translated, "These places where many people die. There is pagoda now for all the people. You go boat only."

"Maybe next time," I answered.

This journey began out of my faithfulness as a sister. After almost thirty-eight years, I walked the dikes near where my brother was killed, but I walked that day more as a mother than as a sister. I walked with my son as my mother was not able to walk with her son. She was not there to hear his last words or to cradle him in her arms. We created an altar of sorts. Out of the gold silk bag came some childhood pictures, a copy of "This is My Song" with verses I had recently discovered, one of the laminated copies of "A Marine's Prayer," a paper crane sent by a seminary friend who emigrated from a war-torn land, two vials of water from the Pacific Ocean, and a few other items.

Hoa brought tangerines and paper money and incense, and we added my incense to hers and divided it into three bundles. She, Luke, and I each took a bundle to light and place in the earth. The smoke began to rise.

So much went up in smoke that day. Of the eight Marines physically wounded that day, I have only spoken to one, Tom O'Connor. One was killed on June 7, 1969. Some have not responded when I or others have contacted them. I have only glimpsed the aftermath, but I know something of its horror: a dead child in Stephen Gregory's path, nightmares that leave men and those who love them shaken, parents who died bitter and before their time, siblings lost to themselves and to one another, energy expended on denying death and guilt and shame instead of affirming life. And it was only one firefight on one day in one war. There is nothing to distinguish it from so many other firefights on any other day. Thirty-nine U.S. troops lost their lives that day in Vietnam. Take any firefight, and the stories are the same. I know nothing about the NVA soldiers killed that day. I don't know the pictures they carried with them or the faces of those they left behind. They have no comrades left these many years later to bear witness or comfort sisters.

Four women working in the rice paddy below came to join us. Hoa spoke with them and they stood in silent witness with us. A few more people came and joined us. One man moved his hand to indicate the verdant landscape and said, "In 1968, nothing green." I turned to Hoa and said, "Tell them this is for all those who died and all the sisters and brothers and mothers and fathers and children." They nodded as they heard her words.

I held Luke as Mom could not hold Bobby, and he held me back. I wanted to use that moment to extract unrealistic promises from him. They boiled down to one thing that I did not ask: "Promise me that you will always choose life."

One bunch of incense caught fire and shot forth flames. "We believe that mean that Bobby here," Hoa said. A few minutes later another bunch flared up. "Maybe Bobby already go other life. He live on," she added.

"Maybe. I know he lives here," I said, pointing to my heart. "And here," I said, pointing to Luke.

"Maybe he tell you not worry about him," she said. I didn't answer. I wasn't worried about Bobby. In that moment I thought of all the other Marines killing and dying. I was worried for them and for all of us. I was worried for the soul of my beloved country. I was worried for all of us who live and die by the sword.

After one batch of incense burned itself out, Hoa told us that the Vietnamese take some of the little sticks from burned incense back to their home altars. For men, the number is seven sticks. She picked out seven sticks for me. Luke then took seven sticks. I poured out water and sand from the beach near my home and put some soil from the dike in the vial.

We left while the smoke was still rising. I followed Hoa and Luke along the dike. The dikes turned, gracefully lacing the rice paddies together. Some places seem consistent with killing and with dying. Large expanses of concrete and steel. Trash laden streets. How many pastoral scenes as beautiful as this hide uglier truths just beneath the surface? How many of our crops grow out of the blood and bodies of soldiers? Grapes in France. Apples in Gettysburg. Rice in Vietnam. Take and eat, you who sleep in peaceful beds. This is my body, broken for you. Take and drink. This is my blood.

Seeking directions

Approaching "The Bobby Place"

Our altar

Leaving "The Bobby Place"

Chapter 26

If the first casualty of war is truth, the last is memory.

Peter Davis

We headed due east back to Highway 1 and turned north toward the Cao Do Bridge, stopping on the south side where Tom O'Connor had been. Bill Ager had met my brother on the north side. Bobby wrote on February 23 that they had moved to the bridge and "hit the enemy before we could be hit. We spotted them moving in position and really tore them up before they could even fire on us." He described setting up in an old French concrete bunker. "I've got a desk, electricity, showers out side. I'm going to buy an ice box and a hot plate, and I'll have it made."

We went on to Marble Mountain and to China Beach and then back along the ocean to Hoi An. Before Hoa departed, she reminded me that if anyone else wanted to go to "the Bobby place," she could take them.

The week before was prelude, and the rest of our time was postlude. We experienced that same restlessness that overtakes people during the postlude in a church service. It is difficult to remember that it, too, is part of the service. The next few days were unstructured with no one to guide us. What at first seemed exotic now seemed surreal. My brother died here? My parents and brother grew up never even knowing about this part of the world. Neither one of my parents traveled beyond Hawaii, yet they raised a boy who died on this oh-so-foreign soil.

We mostly walked the streets of Hoi An. It is known for its tailors, so I brought a minister's stole with me to be used as a pattern for duplicates. At one shop, I noticed a stole on a nearby chair as I paid for my purchases. The woman saw my glance and picked up her reversible stole and said, "I make one for me. Wear to party!" I guess she thought if I wanted several, they must be the height of fashion. I loved the idea of a stole with our symbol of a flaming chalice at a party in Vietnam. Blessings one and all.

I bought my first-ever pain au chocolat and thought of Proust's Madeleine as I was transported back to my first trip to a real bakery. It was the summer of 1964, when I was eleven and Bobby was nineteen. Our family swapped houses with a family that lived on the seventeen-mile drive in Carmel, a few hours south of San Francisco. Bobby had his own car and headed into San Francisco to stay with our Aunt Louise and her husband, Deon, in their apartment in Pacific Heights. After a few days, I joined him, and he was excited to share some of what he had found. We went up and down hills in his Volkswagen and parked in front of a bakery.

It surprised me because Bobby was fairly indifferent to most food, a quality that set him apart in the family. Our small town didn't have a bakery yet, and it was my first visit to one. We worshipped at each glass case before choosing napoleons and chocolate éclairs. It was as if the woman, in official dress, understood the sacred nature of our purchase. She nestled each piece in tissue paper in a pink box and then tied it with a piece of string.

I carried the box in my lap adjusting it appropriately so the contents remained undisturbed as Bobby navigated the car with the stick shift up hills and down them again. We rode the elevator with the ornate metal door up to my Aunt Louise's apartment and placed the box on the dining room table. Greater care was never taken in placing an object on an altar.

Luke and I spent an afternoon at the local orphanage. We brought comb and mirror sets and balloons for the kids and other things on the orphanage wish list. We joined others from around the world for a Vietnamese cooking class, where we ate lunch with two sisters from Australia. As we parted, one said, "I've met a lot of Americans but I've never met one who thinks like you. Individually, they have all been quite lovely, but collectively, they are down right dangerous." When I told this to an Irishman on the boat back to Hoi An, he bent over in laughter and said, "Ah, those Aussies get right to the point, don't they?"

We flew onto Ho Chi Minh City, still Saigon to most. We toured the War Relics Museum where the theme of dangerous Americans was repeated, although not in the way I expected. The displays, while totally overlooking the brutality of the Viet Cong and North Vietnamese, clearly showed the tremendous suffering of soldiers on all sides and especially the suffering of civilians. One section featured the pictures from the book *Requiem: By the Photographers Who Died in Vietnam and Indochina*. Many of those pictures were already etched in my mind, including the one that brought me to a stop and almost to my knees. It is the one by Larry Burrows of a young Marine, alone in a supply shack, weeping.

It was not the exhibits that accused the Americans so much as it was the remarks written by visitors from around the world. I flipped through the pages and saw entry after entry criticizing the United States of America, mostly from our "allies" in Iraq. A typical one read, "Obviously the lessons of Vietnam have not been learned by America today! Shame! Shame! Shame!"

Tired and more than a little cranky, we boarded our flight, ready to be home.

Chapter 27

Better to do a kindness near home than go far to burn incense.

Japanese Proverb

On Saturday, February 10, I sat down with a cup of coffee and powered up my laptop just as the phone rang. It was Tom Hobbs. He emailed earlier in the week and told me he planned to call. I wrote Tom and Jane a year before my trip but got no response. Tom and I passed only a few short emails back and forth since that first four-hour meeting in Westlake Village. As soon as he wrote that he wanted to talk, I felt a sense of relief.

I gave him an overview of my impressions of Vietnam. When I spoke of the old man pointing out the places where "many people die," Tom said that in November, 1968, there were seven battalions west of there.

"How was it for your son?" he asked.

"Luke is pretty quiet. He mostly keeps his own counsel, but he was clearly moved the morning we went to that area, and I had no idea whether he would be or not. He and my mom were close, and I think that was another way into it for him. Since coming back, he has spoken about the orphanage and our experience at Friendship Village. We discovered that Luke and our Hanoi guide were the sons of enemies. I think that was a sobering thing for him to consider."

It seemed to be sobering for Tom as well. "I will have to think about that. I've thought about going with my sons. I think it would be good for them to understand service to your country...."

"More importantly, it might help them understand what it meant to you, Tom, and how it shaped you."

I asked about his family. His sons are both in Austin and doing well. "I have a new grandbaby, a girl. It's not that I didn't want a girl; it's just that I don't know what to do with a girl. With a boy, I could just cuff him upside the head and say, 'Now that I have your attention...' I can't do that with a girl."

"You just lose your heart to her, that's all."

"Yes, that is right," he said, laughing. Getting Tom to laugh always feels like a victory of sorts.

We spoke about Iraq and the similarities. Tom said, "One similarity is that in both you had men doing a job they shouldn't have been doing—McNamara in Vietnam and Rumsfeld in Iraq. They wanted to fight the war. People want to give the military ambiguous instructions and then second-guess them. If you have a clear military objective, the Marines can do what it takes and whatever it takes. That doesn't mean that every objective can be accomplished militarily. Economic, educational, diplomatic, political means also need to be used. You can't abandon those once you start using the military. You need to know the 'end state' you want."

I spoke of the guys who have expressed anger at protestors and told him that Bonnie and I were both protestors.

"I don't like protestors," he said. "You can't have Marines second-guessing what they are doing. You can't have the enemy thinking he can break the will of the people."

The enemy certainly knew that in Vietnam. I thought of the tributes to American protestors at the Hanoi Hilton and at the War Relics Museum. Although the North lost the Tet Offensive militarily, they knew it turned the tide of American opinion against the war and that if they could just hang on, they could win.

I said, "But when we are sacrificing young men for less than clear or honorable objectives, it puts everyone in a bad situation, and the former Marines I know speak more disparagingly of Robert McNamara than the former protestors I know. I've heard Marines express a desire to do things to McNamara that not only violate the Rules of Engagement but the Geneva Convention and maybe even the laws of physics. I think he is proof that intellectual intelligence will never save us."

We both chuckled.

"Well, you guys are all over the political spectrum and have different views on protest too," I said. "About the only thing the Vietnam veterans I know have in common is that they are all Vietnam veterans."

There is great political diversity among the veterans, but a certain attitude is generally assumed, and those who are not in agreement either stay away from gatherings (for this or other reasons) or usually remain silent to keep the peace. As one guy wrote me, "It's lonely on the left with these guys." If someone raises a question, as I have, only then is there a warning about staying away from discussions about "religion, politics, or ex-girlfriends."

"One guy did tell me that he fantasized about coming home and shooting protestors," I said. "But my view is that no matter what our differences, we have something more important in common."

"That's a good way to put it," he said.

"Now, if we can just get the human family to see it that way," I replied.

I told him about seeing Bill Ager and our conversation about guilt and the greenness of lieutenants.

"We didn't start with clear objectives, and they kept changing," Tom said. "There were steep learning curves at every level. Second lieutenants were always green in Vietnam. After four months, they were usually rotated out. As Company Commander, I remember looking out at a hundred and eighty men and wondering what

I got myself into. Then I realized that I just needed to concentrate on my four Platoon Commanders and my XO. The training we got was like training people to swim by having them watch videos and study different strokes, but never getting them in the water. Nothing can prepare you for putting yourself in harm's way. Nothing. Absolutely nothing. I do think officers are better trained today."

I mentioned the book *One Bullet Away: The Making of a Marine Corps Officer*. Nathaniel Fick, a Dartmouth graduate, wrote about serving in Afghanistan and Iraq. "He talks about learning about how free-fire zones[1] in Vietnam were later acknowledged to be 'immoral and counterproductive' but he found himself in a declared free-fire zone in Iraq," I said.

"I'll never forget the look in the eyes of Kilo Company men after that day," Tom said. "They all wanted revenge. As the Company Commander, it was up to me to make sure that the desire for revenge didn't rule the day. You can use it but it can't take over."

"No emotion can rule?"

"That's right."

I told him about the quote from Caputo's book about "sleeping in peaceful beds." We were both silent for a moment. "I think people who don't understand Haditha and situations like that should have to read that book," I said. And then I asked about what had been on my mind since our first meeting.

"Tom, it is good to talk to you. I have worried a lot about the toll that conversation may have had on you and Jane and not hearing from you just increased my concern. Did you regret our conversation? How was it for you?" I asked.

"It's kind of been good. I don't want to talk about it and I want to talk about it. The reason I don't want to talk about it is—"There

---

1   A free-fire zone is an area where everyone is presumed to be an enemy. It is
     OK to shoot first and ask questions later. Or not.

was silence and his voice broke before he finished. Then, he continued. "It's an emotional issue. We had a saying that people who came back and talked a lot about the action weren't in it. I don't even remember what I said that day. I was just reliving it. I think I was probably all over the place. How can you talk about it to people who weren't there? I would look over at Jane's face and her eyes were all big."

"And yet I think she came to understand more about you in those four hours than she has in some years," I said.

"Yes," he agreed.

"You know that I'm writing about this," I said.

"Yes, I don't know how you can and how you will put it all together."

"I'm not sure myself, but one chapter is about my being warned that some things are better left buried, and my belief that we can go back and achieve some healing."

"It's not about closure. It is really opening things up," he said.

"That's exactly what I have said. My ex-husband said he didn't know whether to blame me or thank me but having Luke and me go to Vietnam opened up a lot of things for him. I'm also aware that, in addition to real relationships, you guys symbolize something for me and I think I symbolize something for a lot of you guys."

"You are opening up something we can't open up ourselves," he said.

Oh, Tom, that is what you and your Marine brothers have done for me. And in that opening, may there be new possibilities. And may each and every one of you sleep in peaceful beds.

Chapter 28

I imagine one of the reasons people cling to their hates so stubbornly is because they sense, once hate is gone, they will be forced to deal with pain.

James Baldwin

On a Monday night in late September, 2007, I got an email from Clarence Belgarde telling me he wanted to talk to me about my brother before the upcoming Battalion reunion in Charleston, South Carolina. I didn't recognize his name, but he said he was at the Kilo Company reunion. I sent him my phone number and the phone rang within thirty minutes.

"I don't really believe in PTSD, and I'm not sure exactly how to tell you what I am going to tell you," he said.

"Just go right ahead and say it," I replied.

"Well, I was out bailing hay a few weeks ago, and I saw John Boyce. I thought he died the day I was wounded, but I guess he died the next day. Anyway, I told James Henry about it and he said that usually when you see someone who has passed that in Chippewa tradition that means they are coming to get you. He said there is Indian medicine for that, but after my time in Vietnam and working in ambulances and the hospital here, I figure that when your time is up, it is up. I got hit in the neck and thrown onto a chopper by an arm and a leg in the middle of a firefight, and I lived. So, the next day, I'm out there again and I see him again and he says that all the Kilo Company guys who died are going to be at the reunion memorial service and then he says to me, 'Get in touch with Jan and let her know."

"A ghost told you to call me?" I asked.

"Yep."

"Has anything like this ever happened to you before, Clarence?"

"Only once, when I was in Nam. I was leading us down a trail and a guy appeared and pointed for us to go in another direction and we did and we avoided an ambush," he said.

"A guy who had died appeared?"

"Yeah. Yeah."

Clarence described how shocked and upset he was after seeing John Boyce in the hayfield. "I have three stents, and after this happened the doctor was talking to me about doing a stress test and I said, 'I've already had one.'"

"So how did you know that I am the Jan the ghost was talking about? I don't remember meeting you at the reunion."

"You are the only Jan I know, and I found you by looking through all my old emails from the guys."

It was not until later that I realized it had taken weeks for Clarence to make the connection between the Jan that John Boyce mentioned and the Jan who was at the reunion.

"Clarence, this is an amazing story, but I wasn't planning to go to the Battalion reunion," I said.

"Neither was I until this happened. Now I've sold off some cows and I'm going," he replied.

"Well, Charleston, South Carolina, is a long way from Ventura, California," I said.

"I'm about two hours from Minot, North Dakota, near the Canadian border," he answered. "Anyway, I was just supposed to tell you, and I have."

"I appreciate it. I'll let you know what I decide."

Just when I thought this journey couldn't get any stranger, it had. Instead of thinking that I was writing a book, I suddenly felt like a character in a book being written by someone else—a really strange and interesting book. I thought back over the chapters I had written so far. The last line of this book couldn't be, "And, since it would have been inconvenient, Jan declined to make the trip, however tempted she might have been." I bought a ticket to Charleston, South Carolina.

The Marine motto is Semper Fidelis which translates as "Always Faithful." Most of the men end their emails with "Semper Fi" or "S/F" and I sometimes end mine with "Always Faithful" or "A/F." Lou Buell refers to me as "Always Faithful." We are all faithful, but to whom or to what? When this journey began, I would have said that my faithfulness was quite different from Marine Corps faithfulness. I would have said that theirs is a blind faithfulness, while mine is a questioning faithfulness. I would have spoken about the differences in how we view doubt and ambiguity, but what I have learned has both surprised and humbled me.

Marines have a commitment to leave no body behind. For these men, it meant that they risked death to haul a body out of a rice paddy. My mom used to say, "Do not spend money on me when I'm dead. Wherever I die, dig a hole under me." I would have also taken this to mean that I shouldn't risk my life to haul her body out of a rice paddy.

Once I said to Tom O'Connor, "I can't imagine that my brother would have wanted someone else to risk their life to retrieve his body. I would hate to think that others might have died to do that." He looked at me as if he didn't know where to start, because I just didn't get it. He was right. But now, I get it. Everything hinges on what we are willing to do for one another. Our willingness to sacrifice ourselves to protect one another is everything. We are all in this together. We are all we have. We are the saviors we've been waiting for.

Another time, I said to Tom, "I can understand how officers were afraid and how their own desire for survival took over." Again, he looked at me with incredulity and said what several others had said, "How can you do that when people are counting on you?"

The greatest sin is to put your own safety above the safety of others, and the higher your rank or the greater your privilege, the greater the sin. Les Levy said, "There is nothing more despicable than an officer who puts his own safety first." When we put our own safety first, we are lost and so is everyone else. There is no such thing as individual salvation. We are lost or saved together. When we know that others will put our safety before theirs, all things become possible.

There is another part of "leave no brother behind" that illuminates Marine faithfulness. You are part of something greater, which began before you and will go on after you. You enter into a stream of history, and you will be remembered. You are part of a living tradition. Your memory and your sacrifice will not be in vain. Your Marine brothers will continue to carry you with them, whatever the cost.

And my brother's Marine brothers have continued to carry him and others who made the ultimate sacrifice. While still in the midst of war, these boys and young men contacted family members of killed and wounded brothers. They sent their own family members to visit the sick and wounded. They came home and named sons after fallen brothers. They made pilgrimages to The Wall just to touch a name or to leave a picture or some dog tags saved for decades. Jack Stubbs tends the nearby graves of the two brothers who were Corpsmen. In 2000, Chris Giordano placed an ad in a Louisville paper to find family members of Charles A. Smith, with whom he shared a foxhole for two months. In 2007, he drove 2,400 miles to attend the memorial service of the man who was at his side when he awoke after losing his arm. Another part of Marine faithfulness is that the right thing is not always the easy thing, but you do it anyway. A sister calls you, and you answer. It doesn't matter if you have never spoken of that day, you will now.

We need one another, and others are in need of us. We owe others a debt of gratitude that can never be repaid; it can only be honored. Doing the right thing often requires sacrifice. It is not always easy. We do it anyway. I can sadly say that the United States Marine Corps did a better job of teaching my brother those lessons than the religion of his childhood.

It is easy to say of Marine faithfulness: "Well, that sort of thing requires an enemy. It requires not questioning authority. It requires brainwashing people. You have to get them young." At least it has been easy when I have said these things. It's been easy for me to denigrate sacrifice based on what the sacrifice is for and to even lull myself into believing that sacrifice and extremism of some sort always go together.

I have often trivialized what people are willing to do for their faith because I have not respected that in which they put their faith or the ways in which others take advantage of that faithfulness. But peace and justice require as much or more sacrifice as war, and until we are willing to sacrifice for peace and justice and until we understand that our own well-being is tied up in the well-being of others, our sacrifice will be for war and not for peace. Peace, too, requires faith. My brother's Marine brothers have taught me about the faith needed for peace.

Do we want people who are willing to kill for us? Do we want people who are willing to die for us? Most Americans, I think, would answer yes to both. I would certainly answer yes to the second question. I want people who will stand in resistance to violence even if it means their own death. I want people who will risk their own lives for the lives of others, whether that means rescuing them from fires or raging rivers or from disease or from genocide. If we answer "yes" to either part of that, then how can we not ask what we owe them *before* we ask that, *while* we are asking that, and *after* we have asked that? How can we not ask what we are willing to give in return? If we want people who, when the time comes, will not ask those questions, we owe it to them to ask those questions before we ask them to risk everything.

We owe those going into war a public dialogue about our national interests and our role in the world and our responsibilities as global citizens. We owe them an educated, involved citizenry and well formulated foreign policy with clear objectives. We owe it to them to identify our mistakes, to learn from them, and to take steps not to make the same mistakes over and over. We owe them our own willingness to sacrifice for peace and justice and for a world in which ideological warfare is obsolete.

If we are going to spend months preparing young people to kill and to die, we should be prepared to spend equal energy and resources on helping those who return reintegrate into the community. We owe them tangible forms of support.[1] And that's just for starters.

Although demonizing the troops has fallen out of style, it is still acceptable to demonize policy-makers and protestors and anyone who doesn't agree with us in our efforts to *really* support the troops. Some who have been anti-war activists finally understand that being a peace activist is different than being an anti-war activist, but, for the most part, we haven't made much progress in learning that it's not *who* or *what* we demonize, but *that* we demonize, that is the problem. I have been on websites of so-called defenders of America and defenders of our troops who wish death and destruction to those who hold my ideas and values with rhetoric every bit as vehement as Osama bin Laden's, and I find them even more terrifying because they already live next door.

Just because protestors learned not to demonize the troops doesn't mean we have individually or collectively learned to support our troops. Seeing people as sheer victims or as pure

---

1   In my home state of California, it is estimated that we have 49,724 former members of the Armed Services living on the streets. (*Ventura Star*, November 8, 2007, A4)

heroes is patronizing, and the damage done by either approach is often more subtle and pernicious than when we demonize people.

For years, I saw my brother as purely a victim. He was young and he was trained, even brainwashed, to answer his country's call to battle and, in spite of any doubts he had, that is what he did. If mistakes were made, it was a collective mistake. It was the country's mistake, not his. This was easier for me to believe. But isn't that patronizing to my brother whom almost everyone remembers as one of the smartest people they ever met? He had many opportunities to take himself out of harm's way, and he didn't, even though he had doubts about what he was doing. And there are brilliant young people who make decisions to answer their nation's call to battle who believe fully in the cause or in their duty to answer that call without questioning it. Are they purely victims?

Part of the American mythos is that we create our own reality and that we are all free agents in the game of life. We receive good information, and we make choices after considering a myriad of options and the likely consequences. If we can tell right from wrong, then we are responsible for our own actions. If we chose a certain action and it doesn't turn out well, we will learn from our mistakes and chose a different action in the future. It seems so obvious. Our system of justice is based on this concept. This is why we think punishment is merited and that it will be effective in changing behavior. If we do not have good information, if we do not have a myriad of options, or we are not free to choose, or we don't know right from wrong, or we do not know how to make ethical decisions, then the whole system is called into question.

Those who easily identify victims are sometimes called liberals or even "bleeding heart" liberals. People who take the other approach are sometimes seen as conservatives or even "boot strap" conservatives. Could it be that the truth is much more complex and that we are both shapers of our realities and shaped by a strange mix of conditions and realities, both subtle and obvious? Are we not both object and subject? Might we find a way to acknowledge the complexities of human existence and thus understand individual and collective accountability in new ways that do not deny the power of social structural realities, the hard-wiring of our brains, or the existence of human agency, but use what we know about all of them to build the common good instead of excusing or perpetuating evil?

My brother wrote many times about the overwhelming needs of the children and about giving away more food than he ate or having his Corpsman care for the children. He would have put himself in harm's way for any child. He would have hacked through a jungle to rescue a child or to deliver life-saving medicine. We could have asked him to do that, but we didn't. We could have asked him to become a doctor or to make impossible rescues, but we didn't. We asked him to kill and to die, and we all share the responsibility for what he did and what he didn't do and for his death.

The opposite of demonizing someone is to see them as a hero, but they are just different sides of the same coin. On one side, we project pure evil onto the person and on the other, we project pure good. They are both fantasies and keep us from seeing another person's full humanity or our own. We love to see people as heroes in this country and we love to flip that coin and have it land on villain.

The men I have met do not see themselves as heroes. Many are understandably proud that they answered their country's call and a few are understandably sorry that they did. The one who told me he fantasized about coming home and shooting protestors didn't expect to be treated as a hero. If anything, the protestors reminded him of the guilt and shame he was already fighting, and it was easier for him to turn his rage on them than on himself. And yet, it hasn't saved him from doing that, because in the next breath he said, "If anyone tells you they didn't do something they are ashamed of, they are lying. I will never be finished with this war until I breathe my last breath."

Mostly we want young people willing to lose their innocence while we maintain ours. We want to be protected from the consequences of our decisions and our actions even though the heart of the ethical life requires that we understand and take responsibility for the consequences of our actions. We don't want to even hear what it has meant to our young people to lose their innocence. We do not want to hear the shame or the anger or the sadness. We only want to hear the pride so we can sleep in peaceful beds.

What if we welcomed troops back, not as heroes or as demons, but as people who, at our request, gave up their innocence and perhaps much more? What if we saw them as human beings who have seen the best and the worst that the human family has to offer, as people who have come face to face with evil—the evil in their own hearts as well as in the hearts of others and in the collective psyche?

When I returned from Vietnam, Lou Buell wrote me the two words many of our men longed to hear but didn't: *Welcome home.* What if we simply said, "Welcome home"? And what if we then stood ready to listen to the sorrows, knowing it might take years to hear any of them or all of them. The Bible tells the story of Jesus the night before his death. He didn't ask the Disciples to help him escape. He asked them to simply stay awake with him. Even though this request was simple, they didn't honor it. He waked them and asked Peter, "So, could you not stay awake with me one hour?" They answered by nodding off again.

When I first read this, I thought "What a bunch of losers." I thought back on my own times of pain and how difficult it was for some people just to stay awake to it. But then I thought about the times when I have watched the suffering of others and have felt absolutely helpless to fix it. To just be present both to our helplessness and to another's pain takes amazing strength. And I knew that there were times when people did just that for me, and it meant everything, however inadequate just being present may have felt to them. I thought about the almost uncontrollable desire I have during such times to call on platitudes, religious or otherwise. This is why my chaplaincy supervisor warned us about closing with a prayer. "It's too neat and tidy. It's too tempting to just wrap it all up in a neat little package. You need to find the pain and stay in the pain."

During that hospital chaplaincy, a young man who was just beginning the program was assigned to be with me for the day and to take a break at some point to finish some paperwork. That was the morning the toddler died in her own driveway. After excruciating moments with her parents in a little room designed for just such moments, I offered to take them into the trauma room to see their baby. Just after we went in, the young man took me aside and told me he thought it was a good time for him to go do that paperwork.

Sir Laurens van der Post was a writer, filmmaker, statesman, and anthropologist held by the Japanese as a prisoner of war during World War II. In a video about his life, he told the story of witnessing the execution of two fellow prisoners. One was bayoneted to death and the other was beheaded. Many prisoners fainted at the sight. Van der Post wanted to look away and could have easily looked at the sky, but a voice told him that to look away would be a betrayal of the man being killed. He had to look and to "go through it with him."

Only now do I second-guess my decision, the decision of all of us, to walk out of the cemetery with the casket still poised over the hole in the ground. Recently I officiated at the service for a baby born months early. The hole was so small that a collective gasp went up when it was uncovered. The parents and family left when the service was over. I understood. They had already born witness as I had not been able to do when my brother died. I was grateful for the chance to sit and watch the lowering of that little casket, to bear witness, as I had not done in 1969.

Wars change those who fight them. It has always been thus. How could it be otherwise? As the guys say, "Some gave all; all gave some." Vietnam vets got painted with the PTSD label as if they were experiencing a new phenomenon, as though they, unlike men from all previous wars, just couldn't suck it up and get on with life. PTSD was just a new name for an old horror that wars have always created in the hearts of those who fight them. It has been called by different names, but it is a sickness of the heart, whatever its name.[2]

To prepare them for war, the mindset we have to create in men often undermines their capacity for healing after the war. What if we began with the first question asked by a restorative philosophy of justice: What are the hurts? What might happen if, without placing blame, we simply came together in this country to speak of our hurts from that war of over forty years ago? And what if then, after shedding an ocean of tears and letting our own hearts break again, we listened to the hurts in Vietnam?

Perhaps the most important work of our lives is to go back and reclaim what we have left behind, to make it new and to let it make us new. Going back can change the way we go forward. The meaning of my brother's death is still being written. It is being written by me and by all of us. It was never my intent to make peace *with* my brother's death. It has always been my intent to make peace *out of* his death. And going back helped me understand what that requires.

Here are the articles of my faith, the foundations of the faith that has been reinforced these last few years: Fear is the opposite of faith. When we act out of fear, we are in danger of inadvertently creating what we most fear. My faith is in the power of love and acceptance. It is in the understanding that we are already

2   See Penny Coleman, *Flashback: Posttraumatic Stress Disorder, Suicide, and the Lessons of War*. Boston: Beacon Press, 2007.

connected. Faith is not the same as belief. It is a radical openness to possibility and truth. It is an ability to live well in uncertainty and in mystery.

That a few years ago I knew none of these people means little. We could have passed one another as total strangers and not known, but the connection was there. And that is true for each of us and everyone else. We pass others every day without feeling the deep connection that is already there. And in spite of all of our differences, we share many more things in common. And when we honor those connections, when we honor the similarities, when we risk a change of heart and mind by listening to *the other*, new life becomes possible.

In the end, most of the saving in the world isn't through acts of physical heroism. We don't always have to throw ourselves on a grenade to save a life. Sometimes it can be as simple as being a great big brother. Think that's not a miracle? Listen, this is how it was. When I was afraid of drowning, he calmed the waters. To show me what was possible, he walked on water. He taught me to believe that I could walk on water, too. I felt wholeness in his presence. When I spoke, he listened. He is with me and with others still. He lives. Death is not the final word. Out of the ashes, life again and again and again.

Semper Fidelis.

Epilogue

In the legacies of the dead, we find the seeds of life. in our unfinished business with those we love, we find the core of ourselves.

Krista Taves

Clarence and I sat on the bench seat at the back of the bus on the trip to Parris Island for the memorial service. Seriously sleep-deprived, I counted on the frigid air to keep me awake during Clarence's continuous narrative. He mostly spoke of things he doesn't understand. When he spoke of his son's suicide, tears came out of the corner of his eye and travelled horizontally along a crease in his face until he captured them with his bandana.

We were separated when we went into the chapel, and I sat next to Ed Doyne, who was videotaping the service. It wasn't until the service was over that I realized Clarence was sitting at the end of that pew, which was second from the front. Clarence stepped out of the pew into the aisle and a young Marine, who participated in the service, immediately stepped forward and asked, "Sir, are you okay? Sir, are you okay?" When I approached and put my hand on Clarence's shoulder, the young Marine stepped back.

"Did you see them?" Clarence asked me. "They were all there when they played taps. I know we are not supposed to salute unless we are covered, but they saluted us, and so I saluted them."[1] He buried his face in his bandana.

---

1 Being "covered" means wearing a hat.

On the way back, Clarence told me of his plans to erect a plaque in the little stand of trees that runs between the hay fields where he saw John Boyce. The property owner's son gave him permission saying, "Yeah, my dad has had some experiences in that area, too."

"I still don't understand the connection between John Boyce and your brother," Clarence said.

"Well, if you believe that people who have passed away can be in contact with the living, I don't think it's much of a stretch that John and my brother might be in contact. Plus, I can imagine my brother seeking him out and saying, 'Look, I've tried everything I know to get in touch with her and it isn't working. Don't you know someone who could get a message to her?'" We laughed.

Later, we sat on a couch next to each other in the lobby of the hotel. Looking straight ahead, Clarence said, "I called you, and you came."

"Yes, Clarence, I did."

"I'm glad you did," he said.

"So am I."

Clarence's tribute, placed on his own property, where John Boyce later appeared.

L to R: Les Levy, Jan Christian, Glenn Keith, Jeanne Waldinger, Pete Waldinger, and Tom O'Connor in 2008. *Courtesy of Jack Watson.*

L to R: Arturo Alvarez, Tom O'Connor, Jan Christian, Ed Doyne, Pete Waldinger, Les Levy, Glenn Keith (kneeling in front)

Acknowledgments

On April 11, 2009, the fortieth anniversary of my brother's death in Vietnam, I left a message for Tom O'Connor. Tom calls this "our anniversary." Bill Ager called to let me know that he is thinking about me and my son. Just the month before, there was an email from Ron Watson, whom I have never met, telling me that he "never served under a better person." I am to drop him a line if I ever need anything. "I owe this to your brother and his family for the rest of my life!" he writes. So, the journey continues. Perhaps the most surprising thing for me is how many people who have shaped my life and this story are not mentioned in these pages. I hope you know who you are and find yourselves between the lines.

At the risk of leaving some out, special thanks to:

My son, Luke Christian, who was with me every step of the way in Vietnam and a calm and true presence.

All those who support the Unitarian Universalist Church of Ventura with their time, talent, and treasure. They shared the journey and made it possible.

My colleagues in the Pacific Southwest District Chapter of the Unitarian Universalist Ministers Association who first asked me to share my journey with them.

Andrew Todhunter, an extraordinary teacher, who spent extra time with me at the Mendocino Writer's Conference, told me it was "truth-telling we need to hear," and inspired me to go home and cut about 10,000 words. And then he asked to see a picture of my brother. Every subsequent conversation improved the book.

Claudia Hoffman, who helped with editing and formatting and those little things that can seem so large to someone who doesn't dwell in those details. She declined payment saying, "This was our war and these are our guys."

Margaret Seawell, who shared both her attention to detail and her appreciation for the larger themes.

All who listened to the stories and had faith in my ability to write this book. Some, like Sally Denton, Steve Chawkins, Catherine Rossbach, and Jane Hulse, also offered advice along the way.

Drew Story, who created a website for the book (www. sistersmemoir.com) long before it was finished, which provided inspiration and motivation when it was sorely needed.

The *Ventura County Star* for their ongoing hosting of the videos from our trip on their website (click on "Related Links" on my website to view them).

Helene Atwan at Beacon Press who said, "Go write the book you need to write."

Ed Doyne, the first Kilo Co. brother to read the book, for his encouragement and for letting the book get into his bones.

Shelah Wilgus, for preparing the photos for publication.

And finally to all of those, known and unknown to me, who are keepers of the memories. I would love to hear from you.

Those of us who preach for a living count on our sermons being more wisely heard than they are spoken. And so it is with this book. I put it in your hands hoping you will bring your own wisdom to what you read and that we will go forward together in new ways.

Always Faithful,
Jan Christian

Breinigsville, PA USA
21 November 2010
249773BV00002B/2/P